Learning Through Practice in Initial Teacher Training

Learning Through Practice in Initial Teacher Training

A challenge for the partners

Della Fish

KOGAN
PAGE

© Della Fish, 1989

All rights reserved. No reproduction, copy or transmission of this publication may be made without written permission.

No paragraph of this publication may be reproduced, copied or transmitted save with written permission or in accordance with the provisions of the Copyright Act 1956 (as amended), or under the terms of any licence permitting limited copying issued by the Copyright Licensing Agency, 7 Ridgmount Street, London WC1E 7AE.

Any person who does any unauthorised act in relation to this publication may be liable to criminal prosecution and civil claims for damages.

First published in Great Britain in 1989 by Kogan Page Limited, 120 Pentonville Road, London N1 9JN

Phototypeset in 10.5/12pt Baskerville by The Castlefield Press, Wellingborough and printed and bound in Great Britain by Billings Book Plan, Worcester

British Library Cataloguing in Publication Data
Fish, Della
   Learning through practice in initial teacher
   training: a challenge for the partners
   1. Teachers. Professional education. Teaching practice
   I. Title
   370'.7'33

ISBN 1-85091-790-6

Contents

Acknowledgements   **9**
Glossary   **10**
Introduction   **11**
  – Improving learning through practice   11
  – The readership   12
  – The present context   13
  – The challenge   14
  – The content and organisation   15
  – The underlying philosophy   16
  – The methods   18

PART 1: INITIAL TRAINING NOW: ISSUES AND PROBLEMS

Chapter 1 **Learning Through Practice: Setting Out the Challenge**   **21**
  – *Defining the challenge*   21
  – *The challenge of professional practice*   22
  – *The challenge of practitioner research and theory*   26
  – *The challenge from current professional training*   28
  – *Refining the challenge: some starting points*   32

Chapter 2 **Partnership in Training: Rhetoric and Machinery**   **34**
  – *The historical context*   35
  – *The history of the rhetoric*   39
  – *The machinery for partnership*   42

Chapter 3 **Professional Perspectives Now: Partnership in a Complex World**   **48**
  – *The present context for learning to teach*   48
  – *Learning professional practice now*   53
  – *Some implications for staff and schools*   55

Chapter 4 **Theory and Practice Now: The Context for Initial Training**   **58**
  – *Theory and practice now: towards some crucial distinctions*   59

- *Some present dilemmas about professional practice* 64
- *Five views of theory and practice* 68

Chapter 5 **Reconceptualising Professional Training: A New Basis for Learning to Teach**   72
- *Some ideas about theory and practice* 72
- *Some approaches to learning through practice* 74

Chapter 6 **Developing a Curriculum for Initial Training: Some Design Issues**   86
- *Three models of course design* 87
- *Seven key issues* 90
- *Course design for initial training* 96
- *Two kinds of model for initial training* 98

PART 2: PARTNERSHIP IN PRACTICE: INTERMITTENT SCHOOL EXPERIENCE

Chapter 7 **Some Basic Moves Towards Partnership: Observation Reconsidered**   103
- *Observation: the practice and some theory* 104
- *Observation: some examples* 107
- *Student perspectives* 112
- *Reflections upon observation* 115
- *The practical implications* 116

Chapter 8 **Cooperative Teaching and Cooperative Learning: Team Teaching as a Training Technique**   118
- *Team teaching: the theory* 119
- *Team teaching without the teacher* 121
- *Perspectives on practice* 125
- *Reflections on the technique* 129
- *Some implications for practice* 130

Chapter 9 **School and College Collaboration: Some Successes and Failures**   132
- *The preparation for practice* 133
- *The main action* 136
- *Some perspectives on the project* 139
- *Some reflections* 142

Chapter 10 **Developing a Double Focus: Teaching and Learning to Teach in Tandem**   144
- *Double Focus: the practice and its theory* 145
- *The participants' perspectives* 150
- *Reflections upon the technique* 156

– *The practical implications* 159

PART 3: SUSTAINED SCHOOL EXPERIENCE: SOME CHANGES IN PRACTICE

Chapter 11 **Partners in Crime: Theory Mislaid**   **165**
  – *The preparation for teaching practice* 166
  – *The class teacher's role during practice* 167
  – *The tutor's role during practice* 173
  – *The student's role during practice* 175
  – *Teachers and tutors as partners in crime* 176

Chapter 12 **A Deliberative Approach: Relocating Practice, or Refocusing Training?**   **178**
  – *Refocusing the entire enterprise* 179
  – *Reconsidering supervision* 181
  – *Issues in assessment* 183
  – *Deliberative supervision* 185

CONCLUSIONS: REFOCUSING THE CHALLENGE

Chapter 13 **Towards an Agenda for Action: Some Proposals**   **191**
  – *For individual partnerships: some agenda items* 191
  – *For the practical placement: some suggestions* 193
  – *For the training institutions: some ways ahead* 194
  – *For the future: working on a broader front* 196

Bibliography   **198**

Acknowledgements

All extracts from Department of Education and Science publications are reproduced with the permission of the Controller of Her Majesty's Stationery Office.

My thanks go to Don Allen, Chairman of the West London Press, for permission to use material in Chapters 4 and 5 of this publication, which was originally published in 1988 by the Press as *Turning Teaching into Learning* (Fish, 1988). I am also grateful to Jill Haye for encouragement and help towards publication.

Special thanks go to those colleagues – both fellow professionals and students – in Herefordshire and London, from whom I have learnt so much. Particularly, I should like to acknowledge the staff of the schools involved and the Postgraduate and Bachelor of Education students at West London Institute in the years 1982 to 1988, without whom this work would not have been possible. Julian Distin and Laura Hutchings have made a particular contribution to this work.

Thanks also go to friends and family for understanding and support. I am grateful to Joan Dickerson for help with the production of this text and with proofreading. Last, but by no means least, I am entirely indebted to Evelyn Usher for constant patience and encouragement and for extensive help at all stages.

All errors, however, are mine, and all views here expressed are my own and not necessarily those of the West London Institute of Higher Education.

Note

Following traditional educational research ethics, the identity of specific individuals is obscured by the removal of names and, in some cases, the alteration of gender.

All quotations from students' diaries and pupils' work are presented as written.

Della Fish
October 1988

Glossary

ATCDE	Association of Teachers in Colleges and Departments of Education
BEd	Bachelor of Education
BPhil	Bachelor of Philosophy
CATE	Council for the Accreditation of Teacher Education
CBTE	Competency-Based Teacher Education
CNAA	Council for National Academic Awards
CPVE	Certificate of Pre-Vocational Education
DES	Department of Education and Science
GCSE	General Certificate of Secondary Education
GRIST	Grant-Related In-Service Training
HMI	Her Majesty's Inspectors
IT/INSET	Initial Training/In-Service Education of Teachers
LEA	Local Education Authority
MA	Master of Arts
NATFHE	National Association of Teachers in Further and Higher Education
PBTE	Performance-Based Teacher Education
PGCE	Postgraduate Certificate of Education
QTS	Qualified Teacher Status
TP	Teaching Practice
TVE	Technical and Vocational Education
UCET	University Council for the Education and Training of Teachers
practicum	a practical setting specifically designed so that professionals in training can learn to practise in a real but sheltered environment

Introduction

Summary

- Improving learning through practice
- The readership
- The present context
  - professional training
  - the term 'training'
  - three reasons for urgency
- The challenge
- The content and organisation
  - the basic organisation
  - the parameters of the content
- The underlying philosophy
  - two intentions
  - five allied assumptions
  - ten starting points
- The methods

Improving learning through practice

There are on the market a number of handbooks on teaching practice, survival packs for initial training courses, and workbooks for intending teachers. But this is not one of them. It is, however, an attempt to offer teachers, tutors and students working within initial teacher training some means towards improving a central aspect of that training – the processes of learning from and through practice.

This work is not a handbook because it does not see teaching as a series of discrete strategies, skills and concepts, not does it view practice as yielding to a series of pre-learnt routines and procedures. Rather, it regards improving learning through practice as beginning with practice and proceeding by means of investigation, reflection and deliberation.

In classrooms and schools teachers meet many unique and unpredictable experiences, to which pragmatic decision-making is the only possible response. Improving such problem-solving is therefore central to improving practice. And this involves far more than purely instrumental considerations.

It includes entering into deliberation about educational issues.

Such arguments render irrelevant many previous assumptions about the initial training curriculum and about theory and practice. They are one reason why considerable changes are currently being made to initial training courses countrywide, and their significance will become even clearer as the shape of teacher training in Britain undergoes further alteration in the 1990s.

The readership

This book is designed to be of use to three of the four sets of partners currently involved in initial training, and who in a slightly different guise will no doubt continue to be involved in it in future.

These are: teachers (who have never been given the time to think through all of the issues); students (who are coming to professional training for the first time); and tutors (who may wish to reconsider the issues). More specifically it is written for:

- senior staff in schools (primary and secondary) in overall charge of students and of the school's contribution to the training programme, and who will bear even greater responsibility for trainees in the 1990s
- class teachers (both primary and secondary) whose lessons are watched or taken by students, and who will continue to be involved in future school-based training
- college tutors on professional training courses for teaching (primary and secondary, Bachelor of Education (BEd) courses, and Postgraduate Certificate of Education (PGCE) courses) who currently supervise practice on behalf of the college, and work with students in a range of school-based activities and who will continue in future to foster the trainees' learning from practice
- all students in professional training for teaching whose training programme includes various kinds of experience on practical professional placement, and all future trainees who may find themselves attached to schools as licensed teachers with a need for initial training.

This is not, however, to deny that there is a fourth partner in learning to teach – namely the pupils. It is merely to be realistic that they are not a legitimate audience for this work.

A vast number of the issues about learning through practice on practical placement in schools are also relevant across all the caring professions. Therefore, although this book is focused upon training for teaching, it offers examples and analyses successes and failures which should also be of interest to those involved in the training of occupational therapy, physiotherapy, health visiting, chiropody, police work, and social work.

The present context

Professional training

The context in which this book is offered is that of very rapid change both in the caring professions themselves and in the training for those professions.

The late twentieth century has brought numerous pressures to bear from society upon them. Ironically, many of these have treated such professions as if they were simply another form of industrial production. Such pressures include the demand for accountability, good delivery, quality control, evaluation and appraisal. Inevitably this creates tensions between scientific efficiency and humane caring in both professional conduct and training approaches, as well as raising worries about increased centralisation and deprofessionalisation. Certainly in education such centralised control has increasd dramatically, particularly since 1981, with new laws in the shape of Education Acts, requiring new and tighter procedures in almost every part of the teacher's job. Yet there is also a growing unease that procedures themselves do not equip professionals to cope with the complex and unexpected problems of the unique human situations they meet in real life. Procedures, it is argued, trivialise and distort.

Of course, these conflicting positions and worries can be traced back to conflicting value judgements about education and training. They are at the heart of questions about the teacher training curriculum — and indeed about education for any profession.

But pressures on teacher training are exerted in other directions too. There have been in the 1980s radical changes within the teacher-training community. These include recent developments in knowledge and understanding about both the theoretical and practical procedures of professional training (although there is still much that is uncharted). Many trainers are already familiar with these ideas, and some are already part of new courses. But they take longer to become known by the practitioners who currently oversee the practical training *in situ* in schools, and whose responsibilities for this work will increase in future. Such practitioners tend to assume, in the absence of other information, that today's training courses are much as they were during their own training. Some still maintain the irrelevance of theory and the predominance of unexamined intuition. Such notions are antithetical to training, as Chapter 1 attempts to show.

The term 'training'

The term 'training' is used here purely because it is the one with which many readers will be familiar. It refers to the practical *education* of the student or trainee, and is not intended to imply a narrow approach to teaching or a skills-based view of professional preparation. Indeed, one of the challenges of the book is addressed to those who believe that the process of learning from a practical placement is simple and non-problematic.

Three reasons for urgency

It is becoming increasingly urgent that these issues are faced, investigated and debated more widely among the partners in training for three interconnected reasons.

First, we have entered an era in which in all professional fields importance is attached to the idea of partnership in training between the trainers and qualified and practising professionals. Yet little serious thought has been given either to defining the roles of these two partners or to training either of them (the trainers or the qualified practitioners) in the difficult business of helping students to get the most out of practice and of relating it fully in some way to theory.

Second, as has already been indicated, views about methods of professional training, about the significance of learnt procedures, and about the relationship between theory and practice have altered radically in the last ten years. Yet such views and their practical implications are still largely unknown by or unexplained to those who trained at an earlier time, although it is these colleagues who are now (*without*) any additional training) being made more and more responsible for overseeing, supervising, and assessing the practical work of today's students.

Third, government proposals for teacher training in the 1990s (which are an attempt to ensure the delivery of new teachers who will in turn efficiently deliver the National Curriculum) are now provoking an important debate about the format of initial training. One notion which is central to the 1988 proposals is that teachers should be licensed and paid to work in school before any training is offered to them. Such training would then be based upon their current practice. This idea needs careful consideration. It may offer scope for greater practical work. But more does not necessarily mean better. It may allow for more detailed investigation of teaching and learning within the trainee's classroom. But it raises questions about how and where the skills of investigation will be learnt; how and by whom the trainee's learning through practice will be fostered; how theory and practice will be related; and how (or whether) the practical experience will be extended and enriched beyond the instumental into reflection and deliberation. It may solve some problems about assessment. But it will certainly raise others. It may allow practical experience to be gained by accretion. But bad as well as good habits may be learnt that way.

There is much here, then, to be debated and much to be done. This book attempts to offer some means of engaging with these vital issues and provides some basis for the kind of deliberation that ought properly to fuel these debates and inform action.

The challenge

The challenge here offered to the reader, then, is to enter into deliberation about the issues associated with improving the practical aspects of professional training. By 'deliberation' is meant *not* a casual weighing up of obvious pros and cons, but a systematic enquiry. The following key questions need to be addressed:

1. What is the role of practice in professional training, and can it be improved?
2. What helps students as they attempt to learn through practice, and how can such help be improved?
3. How can those who seek to assist students to learn through practice improve that assistance?

Such questions require all those involved in training to address issues about values, beliefs, assumptions, and theory, as well as about methods of practice. This will involve carrying out investigations into practical work, refining understanding of the problematic issues associated with professional training, and addressing matters of purpose and morality at a deep level, the solution of which cannot be known in advance. The challenge, then, is considerable.

The content and organisation

The basic organisation

The book is divided into three main parts. The first seeks to provide data for deliberating about the role of theory and practice in training for teaching and lays out the challenges that face the partners in professional training (teacher, student, and tutor). These include: issues about learning from and through practice; what is meant by theory and how it relates to practice; what is meant by partnership in training; and issues relating to the design of a teacher-training curriculum.

By contrast, Parts 2 and 3 seek to provide examples of a range of practice in professional training where the partners in training are beginning to work more closely together. Such examples provide the reader with the opportunity to reconsider in context the issues raised in Part 1. These practical examples are provided in two sections.

Part 2 is concerned with intermittent school experience (weekly day visits). Here four examples are offered and analysed of ways in which students can be enabled to learn through practice. By means of these examples issues are raised about: the value of observation; the role in training of cooperative teaching; confusion and failure as well as success in partnership; and Double Focus technique, a special strategy which harnesses the teacher's and tutor's perspectives. These draw on oral and written responses made during the activities by pupils, students, teachers, and tutors.

Part 3 is concerned with block teaching practice (now called sustained school experience) and the student's possibilities of learning from it. This includes comments on the processes of traditional teaching practice and presents procedures for helping students to learn from practice as well as a consideration of ways forward.

The conclusion redefines and extends these challenges for the future.

The parameters of the content

The data provided and the issues explored are related only to those aspects of professional training which take place on practical placements, and in which both the college tutor and the practising professional teacher are involved with the student. This enables close scrutiny of activities which can provide the student with the bases for acquiring practical knowledge, investigative approaches, and reflective and deliberative skills.

Examples are taken from current initial teacher-training courses, both primary and secondary, PGCE and BEd, and refer to the tutor, teacher, and student as the partners, but these have major implications for the detailed operation of the in-service approach to training proposed in 1988 in the Green Paper on Licensed Teachers (DES, 1988). An attempt is made to indicate how such practical experience can be interpreted, extended and enriched via seminars and closely related reading, as this is seen as a vital component in learning from practice. Although it is not possible to present evidence of exactly how such understanding translates into refined practice, the processes of what Schön (1983 and 1987b) calls 'reflection-in-action' are revealed.

In its concern with the student's work in school, this book does not focus on courses which are *only* school-based or placement-based. In fact, it takes the line that only by being embedded in reading, discussion, and other learning activities (which are at present college-based) can the experiences gained in practice be fully exploited for and by the trainee. Indeed, the ability to stand back from the experience with the colleagues who have shared it, but away from the school that provided it, is seen by many as a vital ingredient in learning through practice. Although this book is essentially about practice, therefore, it most definitely does not seek to undervalue other aspects of the training course.

The underlying philosophy

Two intentions

The main aim of this work is to establish a common awareness of the issues and problems of initial professional training, and thus to contribute positively and constructively to the quality of training and the improvement of current partnership in training between qualified practitioners and trainers. The second aim is to offer a contribution towards the establishment of a critical tradition within which the worthwhileness of curriculum proposals and solutions for professional training (both initial and in-service) might be scrutinised. This will become increasingly important as teachers are drawn further into the debate about how best to train teachers. Local committees of the Council for the Accreditation of Teacher Education (CATE), and validating bodies' requirements, demand this now. Imminent future moves over licensed teachers for the 1990s and a new school-based initial training initiative are now opening the debate yet more widely and urgently.

Five allied assumptions

The above statements bring with them an underlying set of assumptions, the most important of which should be acknowledged here as part of the agenda of the book. They include the following:

1. that professional training problems, like all educational issues, are essentially problematic (that is, their solutions will be value-based and not readily agreed) and that recognising this provides the best starting point for addressing them
2. that we need to face more openly how much we do not know about professional training, as well as concentrating on those areas in which we have useful knowledge
3. that among the things that we do not know enough about are the processes which best help students to learn from practice
4. that all knowledge in this area is temporary and is susceptible to refinement
5. that there are many ways of learning through practice, some of which involve doing, some of which involve observing, but all of which involve a range of thinking, investigation, and reading as a vital aid to reflection.

Ten starting points

Against the background that partnership is currently a fashionable means of tackling some of our more difficult problems in society, and that the government requires now, and will increasingly require in the future, teachers, schools, and Local Education Authorities (LEAs) to take a more active part in initial teacher training, the starting points of this book are:

1. a belief in the advantages of the contribution of teachers to initial training, and other professional practitioners to their own forms of training
2. a firm belief that teachers and tutors have allied but differing skills and expertise, and that these differences should not be undervalued or, worse, obscured
3. a persuasion that learning through practice and from practitioners is a more complex activity than is often implied in the way courses are structured
4. a conviction that initial teacher-training curriculum issues should be treated, in the newer tradition of curriculum studies, like all other curriculum problems – as *practical* problems, and thus should be approached via enquiry (see Reid, 1978 Chapters 2 and 3)
5. a deep suspicion that the real and far-reaching practical implications of enquiry-based initial training have not yet penetrated the minds, let

alone the practices, of administrators, nor the consciousness of individuals involved in professional placements and training establishments
6. an allied belief that administrators are, so far, ignoring the demands on two key resources (time and money) which are likely to be made by these new ways of working
7. a belief that even within a deep concern to come to grips with the details of professional practice it is possible to work usefully at two levels of generalisation, and therefore that:
    (a) it is possible to *some* extent to generalise about initial teacher-training courses in spite of whether they are BEd or PGCE, in spite of whether they are for primary or secondary students, and in spite of where they are based
    (b) it is possible to generalise to some extent across the training courses of various allied or similar professions
8. a sense that, at the same time as arguing for generalisation, it is important to provide detail and colour, including quotations from the notebooks and diaries of students on practice, since this is one of the ways forward to exploring these issues
9. a long-term interest in the relationship of theory and practice, which includes a respect for the formal theories of education, as well as a commitment to learning through practice and the uncovering and formulation of personal theory by each individual
10. an interest in the problems of planning courses that bring theory and practice together not only in initial teacher training but also in in-service teacher training and a range of paramedical courses.

The methods

This work itself stands in the tradition of enquiry-based practitioner research, which has so often been used in schools but which has more rarely been applied to the work of higher education. The main approach used was case study. Here the techniques involved keeping field notes and diaries as well as interviewing, using questionnaires and drawing upon students' writing. A survey of practising teachers was also conducted across two London boroughs. The data presented have been collected over a period of five years.

There is no attempt, however, to describe in detail how this research has been conducted, nor to offer critical perspectives upon its methods, and the problems encountered. Instead, the data drawn from these studies are used to raise issues which practitioners can address and investigate for themselves.

Part 1

Initial Training Now: Issues and Problems

1. Learning Through Practice: Setting Out the Challenge

Summary

- Defining the challenge
- The challenge of professional practice
  - what is a professional?
  - what is involve in professional practice?
  - previous assumptions about learning practice
  - their inaccuracy
  - new perspectives
- The challenge of practitioner research and theory
  - practitioner research
  - other British research
  - the international scene
  - the reflective practitioner
- The challenge from current professional training
  - Competency-Based/Performance-Based Teacher Education
  - the Teacher Education Project
  - psychopedagogy
  - the IT/INSET project
  - clinical supervision
  - enquiry-based courses
- Refining the challenge: some starting points
  - learning through practice
  - fostering learning through practice

Defining the challenge

In 1984 Robin Alexander declared that initial teacher training needed a:

> most substantial and necessary shift . . . towards the exploration and use . . . of non-academic, everyday, subjective professional knowledge. (Alexander, 1984, p. 104)

It is becoming clear that this shift is well under way. The arguments used by Alexander, and embraced here too, are not that academic theory should be ditched in favour of practice, but that all practical perspectives which enable students to understand and relate successfully to, and to provide valid educational experience for, pupils are a vital part of teacher training. There is now no doubt that the tide has turned in respect of the acceptance of this approach. But with it have come some new problems about how to give students access to practitioner wisdom and how such knowledge generalises into later practice. In addition to approaches to these matters reported below (Chapters 7 to 11), a range of work is now in progress (for example, Rudduck and Sigsworth, 1985; Busher, Clarke and Taggart, 1988; McIntyre, 1988; Tickle, 1987).

Against this background, then, the challenge for those involved in professional training can be defined as:

the need to come to grips with what can be learnt from practice; how it can be learnt; how that learning best be fostered; and how it ultimately affects later practice.

This challenge to the partners emanates from three major sources:

1. the changing views about professional practice and the pressures upon professional practitioners as a result of society's changing attitudes to the professions (the challenge of professional practice)
2. the changing focus of professional research and the interrelated changing views about professional theory (the challenge of professional research and theory)
3. the changing approaches to professional training courses including the demands about partnership (the challenge from current professional training).

Each of these will now be considered in detail.

The challenge of professional practice

The very nature of professional practice itself issues a challenge to the partners in training to reconsider the content and methods of training. First, however, we must turn to the word 'professional'.

What is a professional?

This question has been raised as a means of ground-clearing, by acknowledging the inevitably problematic nature of all the issues related to teacher training. The question takes us back to what is meant by a profession and whether teaching is a profession. There is no simple answer to this. Some, like Langford (1978, 1985), argue that teaching as an activity might be organised along either professional or bureaucratic lines. Some, like Schön (1983, 1987b), argue that teaching is a minor profession. Some, like Hoyle (1974), look in detail at the implications of professionalism for teachers. Langford makes the point neatly:

> No final decision can be made about whether teaching is a profession without first deciding on the weight to be given to the many different factors involved and there is bound to be disagreement about how to do that. There is certainly no one correct way of doing this even if the proposed definition of a profession is accepted.

(Langford, 1985, p. 63)

What makes all of this more difficult still is that in the present period of rapid change, attitudes to and ideas about professional responsibility are also changing, and with them expectations about what professionals should be able to do.

What is involved in professional practice?

Carrying out professional practice was at one time assumed to be a matter of putting into operation (applying) previously learnt professional theory to a practical situation. But now that practice has come more closely under investigation it is clear that these long-held assumptions are challenged by many of the daily experiences of practising professionals.

However, as Schön (1983, 1987a, 1987b) argues very persuasively, rather than being a matter of applying pre-learnt theory to expected practical situations, the nature of professional practice is unpredictable and does not yield to routine. Professionals, he suggests, cope daily with unexpected, unforeseen, previously unknown, uncertain and unique human situations. To these they are expected to respond, on the spot and immediately. The problem is that the procedures that have been set up, the techniques previously operated, previous knowledge, and preferred routines either fall short of or simply do not fit what is happening.

There would seem to be more unsuccessful than successful responses to this predicament.

At worst such situations evoke four main sorts of unsuccessful reaction:

1. a determined adherence to known and trusted procedures in the face of all odds
2. a pretence that the surprise element does not really exist (and a continued application of known procedures)
3. an expansion of current procedures and control systems to 'nail down' the new problem for next time
4. recourse to intuition and instinct which, being blind and essentially hit-and-miss, are more a matter of luck than judgement.

In the first three of these cases, previously known routines have been the unsuccessful starting point. In the fourth, known procedures have given way to what might be called the 'bran-tub' approach. In none of these cases could anything new have been learnt from the experience.

Arguably, though (and still following Schön), the surprise in the unique situation might successfully be met by starting with the new situation itself, and by seeking to learn from it. Such learning might lead to the evolution not of new and inflexible routines, but to principles for coping with the unexpected, and to a better understanding of how we learn from practice. What might in this case be brought to the problem is a willingness:

– to learn by experiment

- to use a variety of approaches
- to work by trial and error but systematically
- to start with intuition, but to turn it into insight by thinking about it during and after the action.

Here, in other words, the professionals start from practice and enquire into it as they go, systematically, and with a view to learning both about the new situation, and about how to deal with new situations.

If these activities are characteristic of at least some of the daily encounters of professional life, and if, in addition to this, the whole notion of what professionals should be expected to do, both by and for society, is also changing, this raises serious questions for those involved in professional training about how to prepare for such practice.

The implications of this are profound. They suggest the need to abandon much of our recent approaches to learning professional practice. A careful consideration and critique of traditional notions of training offers a useful starting point for exploring this.

Previous assumptions about learning practice

The following ten points might be said to characterise the assumptions underlying traditional training approaches.

1. Learning (the theory) and doing (the practice) are two quite separate activities.
2. Theory must be known before practice can successfully be attempted.
3. Only knowing theory and performing routinely are involved in learning to become a professional or in improving professional practice.
4. The opposite of 'acquiring theory' is simply 'doing action'.
5. Learning and improving practice is merely a matter of repeating routines.
6. What really makes a person 'a professional' is *theoretical* knowledge.
7. This theoretical knowledge, which should be acquired and subsequently applied to practice, is absolute and unproblematic.
8. The mastery of theoretical knowledge will somehow ensure the mastery of practice.
9. The theoretical knowledge about professional practice which is needed by practitioners is available from research and will, automatically, be relevant to the practitioner's practical problems.
10. The onus is upon the practitioner to demonstrate the relevance of the theoretical knowledge. Not to be able to do so is a failure of the practitioner.

Their inaccuracy

Such a set of assumptions has for many years lurked beneath man's view of knowledge, as Gilbert Ryle (1949) has shown us. He characterises it as the myth of the ghost in the machine, and indicates its tyranny over our thinking by referrring to it as 'dogma'.

This dogma has falsely led us to believe that when we do something intelligent we separately 'do' and 'think'. But this is not the case, as a moment's reflection upon any recent intelligent action of our own will confirm. In fact, we usually think and do at the same time and each activity influences and refines the other. Thus, as performer, we take responsibility for that performance by regulating it appropriately in and to the actual situation. This we might call intelligent performance, by contrast to mechanical performance which abandons thinking during action and in which the performer is on a kind of auto-pilot. This whole approach to intelligent performance is commonly acknowledged in our grandparents' phrase 'think what you are doing'.

The mistake here, however, can be to conclude that the intelligent performance in which the performer is thinking what he is doing depends entirely upon his translating previously learnt rules, laws, and principles into action.

This is clearly not so since we can often perform intelligently even when we cannot articulate (or simply do not know) the laws or rules which cover our action. Indeed, such rules are likely only to have emerged in the first place from effective practice by reflection upon it.

Thus, intelligent action has intelligent processes built into its accomplishment, not necessarily intelligent precursors in terms of theoretical argument. As Ryle says:

> What distinguishes sensible from silly operations is not their parentage but their procedure . . . 'thinking what I am doing' does not connote 'both thinking what to do and doing it'. When I do something intelligently, ie thinking what I am doing, I am doing one thing and not two. My performance has a special procedure or manner, not special antecedents. (Ryle, 1949, p. 32)

Practical knowledge (knowledge how), then, stands not in the shadow of theory (knowledge that), but in its own right as the centre of professional practice.

The following can now be argued:

1. Theory and practice, though separate in kind in some ways, are interrelated and become one in practice.
2. Learning to do is achieved by doing, which involves thinking.
3. Practice can usefully precede theory, and theorising is a form of practice.
4. Performance of practice involves more than simply knowing theory and producing a series of routine actions. It involves judgement, decision-making, and improvisation and a pragmatic approach to the particular situation. These in turn are capacities influenced by our dispositions but also related to personality. (There is much here that a professional practitioner needs to explore, and much that we do not yet know about.)
5. Simply repeating the routines of practice is unlikely to improve that practice and certainly will not determine its quality. What is needed is reflection upon the practice, the drawing out of the underlying theory

and the seeking of other theory and/or practice which might enlighten it, together with deliberation upon its ends.
6. Starting with some form of practice might well prove the most effective way of understanding practice as well as of improving it, but practice without reflection (which should be fuelled by a range of sources and fostered by debriefing) is as arid as unrelated formal theory.
7. Mastery of either theory or practice is unlikely to be attained since both are temporary, problematic, and always susceptible to improvement.
8. The knowledge from research which is relevant to practice, though as yet fairly limited, is increasing as professional practitioners research their own practice.

How, then, do these assertions affect professional practitioners and the training for professional practice?

New perspectives

When theory is no longer seen as a precursor to practice, when effective practice can precede intelligent theory, and when both theory and practice can equally be described as intelligent or uninformed, the following perspectives are opend up:

1. Views about how one initially learns practice and learns from and through practice may have to be modified.
2. Procedures for refining ongoing practice may need to be redefined.
3. Attention to practice may become a means of approaching theory and the learner may thus construct and refine her own personal theory of action as well as setting it in the context of wider theory.
4. The relationship between theory and practice during professional training may need reconsideration, especially in respect of assumptions about their temporal relationship during the course.
5. It may become increasingly important for all professionals to consider what is involved in learning or improving something practical.

Professional practice or experience of it are not necessarily *inevitably* beneficial to the trainee, however. It is important to consider what aspects of practice may be useful and how they should be organised in order to become the proper material from which a traineee may learn. The chapters which follow are an attempt towards this.

The challenge of practitioner research and theory

If the nature of professional practice itself represents a major challenge for the partners in training, so do mid 1980s developments in practitioner research and the new theoretical base they are providing for professional practice. While it is not the purpose of this chapter to look in detail at research in the field of teacher education, it is important to recognise that there have been major developments.

Practitioner research

Pre-eminent among approaches to practitioner research in the 1980s has been that designed on the Lawrence Stenhouse model of teacher as researcher. The significance of this approach is that it starts from practice and is carried out by the practitioner. (See Stenhouse, 1975.) While not all of the work reported below stems from this approach, much of it does.

Among this is the work begun at Cheltenham in 1983 and which gave rise to a major conference there on teaching practice (TP) in summer 1986. This work, influenced by earlier studies, has concentrated mainly on the discussion between the triad of teacher, tutor, and student in the post-lesson analysis. (See Terrell, Tregaskis and Boydell, 1986.) The work of Tickle (1987) at the University of East Anglia also offers perspectives on partnership in initial training. The vital processes of debriefing from practice are commonly needed across a range of caring professions, which is why a pilot project, 'How to Enable Learning in Professional Practice (HELPP), is now under way at West London Institute, investigating this aspect of training for teaching and health visiting, with a view to establishing means by which colleagues can investigate these issues further.

But these are only examples of a busy scene which also includes work on practitioner research run by the Cambridge Institute (see Nias and Groundwater-Smith, 1988); the work of individuals like Colin Biott on classroom action-research in initial training (Biott, 1983); and Andrew Pollard and Sarah Tann on teaching as a reflective activity (Pollard and Tann, 1987).

Other British research

Among other work in this field three other research activities must be mentioned. They are Paul Hirst's research, in the early 1980s, into the work of school-based PGCE courses; McIntyre's work on the school-based PGCE at Oxford University (McIntyre, 1988); and Margot Cameron-Jones' work at Moray House on helping students learn from professional practice: the Primary Placement Project (Cameron-Jones, 1987). Hirst's research, which was work on a far wider scale than any other in recent years, unfortunately has not been published to date. McIntyre's work reports a range of research under way, based around the Oxford course. The work at Moray House will not be completed until 1989 but has already given rise to useful materials on assessing teaching practice (Cameron-Jones, 1986).

The international scene

Internationally, the scene is alive with interesting and relevant work about professional practice and training, much of which is now beginning radically to affect training in Britain. Particularly important is the work of Donald Schön (1983 and 1987b); Stephen Kemmis with Wilfred Carr (1986); and David Boud, Rosemary Keogh and David Walker (1985). The work of Kenneth Zeichner (1986) in the United States and Allan MacKinnon (1987) in Canada is particularly useful in investigating reflective practice (see Chapter 12). Of these, the work of Schön on the reflective practitioner is perhaps of pre-eminent importance.

The reflective practitioner

It was Schön who in 1983 first called attention to the major changes needed in professional practice (and by implication training), and to what would arise if professionals became more self-consciously reflective about their actions and 'held a conversation' with their current professional problem (Schön, 1983). Subsequently, he has elucidated the resultant implications for professional training, though he does not use teacher training as an example (Schön, 1987b).

The activities involved in reflection have been usefully delineated by Schön (1987b); Boud, Keogh and Walker (1985); and Pollard and Tann (1987). (For more detail, see Chapter 4.)

The Marxist critique of this kind of work, as being not radical enough or widely enough conceived of as a means of reconstructing society, is provided by Shirley Grundy (1987), and principally by Carr and Kemmis (1986). They also propose a more radical paradigm for investigating practice which, however, has echoes of Stenhouse (1975).

There is, then, a developing knowledge base about practical, professional training, and there are associated major changes in views about theory. These give considerable substance to the claim that current research issues a challenge to the trainers.

The challenge from current professional training

Teacher-training courses have varied enormously across the country, though there are now many constraints upon them from the government and the validating bodies. (See Chapter 6.) Their varied range and scope are the result of the value-based nature of decisions about the initial training curriculum, which even the 1988 Education Reform Act and its implications will not be able to obliterate. Their present differences in emphasis, in terms of theory and practice, signal the challenge to professional trainers to be alert to enter the current debate about teacher training for the 1990s.

This section, then, refers to six different approaches to initial training as a means of illustrating diverse views on learning through practice.

Competency-Based/Performance-Based Teacher Education

At one extreme end of the instrumental approach to teacher education lie Competency-Based Teacher Education (CBTE) and Performance-Based Teacher Education (PBTE). These are approaches influenced by American research into education rooted in behavioural psychology. Here teachers are viewed as technicians who will simply apply what educational research has discovered. The activity of teaching is considered to be exclusively skills-based, and it is assumed that teaching can be analysed, described and mastered. This approach assumes that the baseline of competence to teach can be laid down and teachers can be tested against it before being accepted as qualified teachers. Clearly all of the problems associated with the behavioural approach to learning apply here. (See Clark, 1979, and MacDonald-Ross, 1975.) There are echoes here too of some approaches to teacher appraisal. In Britain C/PBTE is unlikely to be extensively adopted, although the Further Education Unit has recommended it for training for tutors on Youth Training Schemes and training for Technical and Vocational Education (TVE) Schemes.

The Teacher Education Project

Many of the micro-training techniques and other attempts to analyse skills as the basis for training are in many ways similar to C/PBTE. One example of these is the Department of Education and Science (DES)/Nottingham University Teacher Education Project. This was based upon a three-stage model (research followed by the development of training materials and then their trial) on seven broad fronts, which were chosen as being of central concern for all students (on a secondary PGCE course). The work includes workbooks on: classroom management and control; mixed ability teaching; teaching bright pupils; the education of slow learners; questioning; and explaining. These booklets contain three sections: a pre-experience section which introduces the topic via readings and exercises; a teaching practice workbook, based on the premise that several students will work together with a teacher and a tutor on a number of classroom exercises; and a post-experience study text where the issues might be pursued in greater depth.

Again, this project is instrumental in approach, placing skills learning as central. It offers more to the slower student and leaves the quicker ones both impatient with the text's rate of progress towards quickly taken points, and the apparently simplistic assumptions about what is involved in teaching.

Many have a similar reaction to Edgar Stones' claims that psychology should provide the main basis of a theory of teaching.

Psychopedagogy

The main substance of Stones' approach to teaching practice supervision is that across concept teaching, problem-solving and psychomotor skills teaching, there should be a use of teaching schedules which he has drawn up and which are informed by an understanding of learning psychology (Stones, 1984). These schedules are explained at length in Stones' earlier work *Psychopedagogy* (1979), which itself demonstrates how a knowledge of educational psychology can be applied to practice by the teacher.

He argues that there is a range of pedagogical skills currently neglected but fundamental to effective teaching. These, he argues, include assessing baseline competence in any learning situation (the notion of mastery thus rears its head), the ability to analyse the learning task and contingent teaching task, the ability to make diagnostic evaluation of pupils' learning problems, and the understanding of reinforcement and feedback. There are echoes of the National Curriculum here.

Here, then, in the first three examples, we have a clear indication of how training would proceed in the hands of those who regard teaching as a matter of technical mastery. It should be noted that such approaches tend to drive theoretical knowledge back into colleges and practical work into schools. A much wider approach to teacher education is to be found in the Initial Training/In-Service Education of Teachers (IT/INSET) project.

The IT/INSET project

The IT/INSET project was based at the Open University and its funded life extended from September 1978 for three years. The purpose of the project was to 'assist selected training institutions to demonstrate a new concept in teacher education'. (See Ashton et al., 1983, p. 25.) The aims of the project as they appeared in the proposal for funding were:

1. To develop in-service training programmes for schoolteachers based upon procedures for professional self-evaluation and development;
2. To provide a framework for an evaluation and development cycle within each school . . . ;
3. to provide opportunities for students in initial training to develop their competence as teachers through participation in the school-focused activities associated with . . . 1 and 2 above; and,
4. To provide opportunities for the professional development of teacher-trainers through their involvement in school-focused in-service training. (Ashton et al., 1983, p. 18)

The essential nature of the English project (which was linked to other projects in Sweden and Portugal) was that 'of teacher-tutor teams working on areas of the curriculum *which were of concern to teachers*' (Ashton et al., 1983, p. 26, italics mine). We already begin to see, therefore, that the major concerns were focused upon the in-service part of the work. The choice of problem to be investigated is made by teachers and the school, and the investigation is for the school. The assumptions are that the initial training student will naturally gain from working in real schools with teachers and tutors. While this is undeniable, it is also possible that they might learn more from similar work devised with *their* particular education in mind. Further, IT/INSET was implemented mainly in the later years of BEd courses. Thus it can be seen as offering advanced, rather than basic, help with preparation for the classroom. It also seeks to apply Education Theory to classroom practice.

A contrast to this approach, though still concerned mainly with in-service work, is John Smyth's clinical supervision.

Clinical supervision

Smyth's work stands in a long tradition of work carried out in the United States and referred to as clinical supervision. Here, counselling skills are brought to the aid of teachers who are trying to learn from their practice. Work in this field was pioneered by Goldhammer in 1969. For him the term 'clinical' meant 'forms of learning about teaching that were solidly embedded in the daily classroom practices of teachers. (See Smyth, 1986, p. 1.)

The aims of clinical supervision are generally held to be:

- to help a teacher expand his or her perceptions of what it means to be a teacher, through the discovery of strengths and weaknesses;
- to assist the teacher to regularly and systematically examine personal teaching to see if there is a match between *intentions* and *actions*; and
- to provide the teacher with a methodology by which to monitor the effect of bringing about changes to teaching.

(Moore and Mattaliano, 1970, quoted in Smyth, 1986, p. 3)

The method involves a pre-observation conference, where the teacher and observer set out their agenda; observation itself, which involves a careful collection of a pre-arranged range of data; an analysis of the observed activity, done separately by both teacher and observer; and a post-observation conference.

This work does not lend itself as a whole to use in current initial training, although it offers an interesting perspective on starting from practice and how to help teachers to learn from it. It assumes a qualified teacher requires extensive and collaborative work on a one-to-one basis, and is time-consuming. It also seems to rely upon a very rigid routine, which does little to accommodate the problems about the unpredictability of practice which Schön has pointed to.

The approach which must closely accommodates Schön's ideas is to be found in a variety of British enquiry-based initial training courses.

Enquiry-based courses

Such courses spring from the Stenhouse model of action research, which originally involved practising teachers. Essentially, they involve students in investigating practice (their own and others') as a means to learning to teach. They may or may not be exclusively school-based. Such courses take on much of the flavour of action research. They involve students in control of their own learning agendas, formulating their own personal theories about action, and working with teachers and tutors as equal colleagues. But, as Nias usefully points out, this is professional enquiry and not action research. (See Nias, 1988, p. 2.) That is, the enquiry does not normally lead to refinement of action immediately and in the same arena, but rather feeds understanding about action which may guide later practice. Nias and Groundwater-Smith (1988) provide a range of examples.

Professional practice itself, current research into professional practice, and various forms of professional training, then, all point to the same challenge for those involved in training. That is: the need to come to grips with what is involved in learning from practice, and how such learning can be fostered. All three fields also illustrate that there are no simple or ready-made answers to such a challenge, but only a need continuously to refine the problem, our practice, and the means of considering both.

Refining the challenge: some starting points

What, then, do we mean by learning through practice, and how can it be fostered?

Learning through practice

Following Passmore (1980), pp. 69–72, it is possible to distinguish 'learning from practice' from 'learning through practice'.

Learning from practice can be said to involve learning a particular skill or set of skills and a range of associated concepts, abilities, routines, strategies and closed capacities (the ability to do something which can be mastered and may become a habit). Such learning is often achieved via demonstration and observation, carried out with a view to copying and then constantly repeating the activity involved. Its end is to master and reproduce a reliable and efficient version of activity which has been witnessed and experienced.

Learning through practice, on the other hand, can be said to have a very different emphasis. This would involve carrying out some practice or activity but in order to use such learning and experience as a vehicle through which to learn something wider and of more significance. As will be clear, the first of these is usually associated with training for specific skills, and the development of habits and closed capacities. The second (learning through practice) is more central to the enterprise of education, which seeks to open the learner's mind to wider understanding. (See Fish, 1988, p. 64.) Thus, the teacher in training who follows a simple workbook on, say, questioning skills may be able to learn certain skills, techniques, capacities. But the student who investigates the role of teachers' questions in practice may do this and simultaneously be able to attend to the wider and highly significant issues about the educational ends of questioning.

Fostering learning through practice

Clearly there is no way of enabling learners to learn to practice or to learn through practice by means of instruction. Thus, the issue, for the trainers, is about fostering the students' learning and Part 2 and 3 of this book are about these processes. However, we can already make some observations about them.

Doing something yourself and teaching others to do it usually involve differing expertise. This means that professional practitioners themselves are not *necessarily* the best or only people to foster the learning of professional practice. This argument often causes much confusion, and so the statements below are an attempt to illustrate the main points of it.

1. Being expert at something does not necessarily make one good at enabling others to do it.
2. But most people would agree that it is definintely better to have had some practical experiential yourself to draw upon in order to help the learner. How recent, immediately relevant and of what duration this experience should be is of course logically open to question, and is dependent on the expertise of the individual. The *quality* of that experience and the level of the trainer's personal expertise is, of course, more important than the quantity. The natural goodness of practice is a myth, and one that pervades many government pronouncements about teacher training.
3. Equally, however, most people would agree that anyone who had simply been through a period of experiential learning would not yet be ready themselves, as a result of just that, to teach others how to teach it.
4. It is for this reason that everyone who is to become a trainer of others in school needs:
   (a) to have had, reflected upon, and deliberated about a range of practical experience
   (b) to have considered the strategies that are useful for helping others to learn to teach (including the development of the processes of debriefing trainees after practical experience).
5. Teaching and learning are, in one sense, part of the same activity for everyone involved in professional training in that a teacher is always caught up in the concomitant nature of teaching and learning to teach.

Involvement with teacher training, then, necessitates coming to grips with:
- *what can be learnt* through *practice*
- *how it can be learnt*
- *how that learning might best be fostered*
- *and how it affects later practice.*

In doing this, the partners (teacher, tutor, and student) will be engaged in a genuine voyage of discovery since relatively little is yet known in detail about these matters, and since there are no better experts in the field than themselves.

The rest of this book sets out in some detail aspects of the current knowledge base for this work, and deals with some of the implications for the partners in training by reference to some practical examples. First, however, it is necessary to turn to the present government requirements of partnership itself. Interestingly, these requirements see as partners the tutor and teacher, but not the student. It is not yet clear what the 1989 government initiatives will be in this respect.

2. Partnership in Training: Rhetoric and Machinery

Summary

- The historical context
  - post-war pressures
  - early moves towards partnership
  - the re-emergence of partnership
- The history of the rhetoric
  - emerging concern about teacher training
  - *Teacher Training in the Secondary School*
  - *Teaching in Schools: The Content of Initial Training*
- The machinery for partnership
  - *Teaching Quality*
  - *Circular 3/84*
  - *CATE NOTE 4*
  - the life of CATE
  - latest initiatives

Introduction

For teacher-training institutions, partnership between teachers and tutors as part of the process of training is currently a vital issue, since at present they cannot gain permission to run any initial training course unless they can demonstrate the existence of real partnership between themselves and schools. In schools, the content and the extensive implications of these new demands are only just beginning to be grasped. This chapter sets out to present the main requirements of partnership between schools and teacher-training institutions, to consider their implications, and to see how they arose.

Two perspectives are offered. First, a brief historical background is provided, by looking at developments in teacher training over the last 25 years. Second, the machinery which has been set up to ensure partnership in training between schools and the training institutions is considered critically. The need for this machinery was established originally via a number of Her Majesty's Inspectors (HMI) discussion papers, and became a requirement of training by means of government white papers and circulars. The machinery is currently embodied in the CATE in its local and national forms.

The historical context

Post-war pressures

Since the second world war, and particularly in the last 25 years, teacher training in this country has been swung through a series of dramatic changes. It has ricocheted from expansion to contraction. Public sector plans totalled 32,500 in 1960, rose to 114,000 by 1969, fell to 46,500 by 1979, and could be at an all time low by 1992. In the public sector in the 1950s and 1960s teacher training found its base in monotechnic institutions and was validated by universities. In the early 1970s, in the wake of the 1972 White Paper, *Education: A Framework for Expansion*, it bedded down mainly in institutes of higher education and polytechnics with a number of other courses, and mainly Council for National Academic Awards (CNAA) validation. In all of this time, it has been under challenge about its standards and its methods.

One of the major concerns behind questions about balance and phasing of the courses has been about the adequacy of the practical side of the training, and the tenuous relationship to it of theory.

Early moves towards partnership

The history of teacher training from the early post-war period through to the 1970s actually saw many examples of good and useful cooperation between schools and colleges in various aspects of the training course. They were examples which used many methods and arose from many motives. But they rarely sprang from any deeply considered theoretical ideas about theory, practice and how to enable people to learn to teach.

Indeed, it comes as something of a shock to remember that the very questioning of the old divisions of Educational Theory into the four ugly sisters of philosophy, sociology, history, and psychology only began in earnest in the later 1970s. (See, for example, Golby, 1976.) This is a salutary reminder of how far and how fast we have come in some ways in the last decade. Yet even now it is not clear how far such advances are based on a sound foundation.

The notion of partnership between schools and colleges was in existence at least as early as the early 1960s and, ironically, its champions were the college lecturers and not the government. Perhaps the best indication of this can be found in the *Evidence to the Central Advisory Council for Education*, by the association of Teachers in Colleges and Departments of Education (ATCDE), which was published in November 1964. Here, 25 years ago, the ATCDE declared:

> Practical work with children must assume a large role throughout the training of the Primary teacher. It cannot be isolated from the rest of the course nor restricted, for example, to 'block practices' and periods of 'observation' . . . A constant interchange is needed between college and school, students and children. (ATCDE, 1964, para 63, p. 26)

> A real partnership between schools and colleges could result in a far more easy and informal entry for students into schools and hence in a far more profitable and less disturbing relationship with children. (ATCDE, 1964, para 66, p. 27)

Here, then, is clear evidence of positive attitudes to ideas about partnership, but also evidence that these ideas do not bring with them any notions about the complex relationship of theory and practice. But there was no sign from government that it regarded these issues as critical, and there were no additional resources available to encourage this approach.

These very points were already being focused upon by the end of the 1960s when the Twentieth Symposium of the Colston Research Society, held in Bristol in April 1968, devoted its entire proceedings to looking 'Towards a Policy for the Education of Teachers' (Taylor, 1969). Looking back today to those papers, we see evidence of concern about how to educate and train teachers, worries about theory and practice, and the standards of the practical aspects, and, ominously, some comments about the government's role in the debate. The level at which this debate was conducted (within a research symposium run for senior staff within education), however, was somewhat exclusive, and certainly well beyond the majority of those in either the colleges or the schools. This is not to dismiss the symposium itself, but rather to rue the fact that by the early 1970s, when the debate was due to be conducted at the grass roots, the government had made academic standards in teacher training the main focus, and the colleges had their energies caught up in their own struggle for survival.

Yet, in some of the words spoken at Bristol in 1969, we find remarkable echoes of the issues now being faced in the late 1980s in teacher training. For example, in the contribution of Miss Browne, then principal of Coventry College of Education, we can see new ideas for the role of the practising teacher:

> Students will need to get practical experience early in their course, but it should be with children and young people and those in charge of them in playgroups, clinics, youth clubs, residential camps and the world of work as well as in schools. As far as possible it should touch different ages, classes, races and environments. Observation must take place at first hand, but for more exact and repeatable viewing and analysis, film and television will be in normal use. Practising teachers must be called in more than at present to take part in advising and supervising students, but they must help them to evaluate their experience according to principles of education agreed between themselves and the college. (Taylor, 1969, p. 103)

Here, in this last sentence, we have the nub of the issue for today.

Not only do we find a call for developments in partnership between schools and colleges, but we find coupled with it a recognition of the need for the teacher-partners to have a clearer understanding of the theoretical and practical bases for that work. This is the idea that we will need to focus upon if we are to make the 1980s government rhetoric about partnership into something of real substance.

Interestingly, a more ominous note is struck by Edward Britton in his address to the conference, at the end of which he declares:

> At present the DES have effective control over numbers, the length of the training course, the balance between numbers of primary and secondary teachers, and the material conditions in which training is given. They have no control over content and method. In this country we react badly to Governmental control of content and method in any area of education, and quite rightly. But the alternative of leaving content and method to the decisions of twenty Area Training Organizations (the bodies then in control of colleges) with not even a recognized national body to make hortatory noises in their direction is surely going to the other extreme ... I do not believe that there would be one teacher ... who would not agree that the teaching profession should have a much larger voice in deciding the content and method of its own professional training. (Taylor, 1969, p. 189)

One other comment, from the discussion of Edward Britton's contribution, has interesting reverberations. Mr Norman Evans, then of Culham College, declared:

> I am quite sure ... that it's possible to redefine the role of the school from being a site for an operation (for teaching practice) to an equal, probably a senior partner in the teaching practice periods. (Taylor, 1969, p. 199)

The possibilities in and implications of this remark are explored at length in Chapters 11 and 12.

But it was not only at prestigious conferences that some of the recent government ideas were already being explored at the end of the 1960s. At this time also, college staffs were given recognised time to work on their own in schools, if they wished to do so, to improve their own experience, though this was not seen by any official body as an important priority, or even as connected with partnership.

Interestingly, there was no mention of this idea in the Bristol conference. Indeed, it depended purely on the policy of the individual college. For those who did involve themselves in this work, the assumption was that college staff should simply widen their own private, practical experience (just as they were also being encouraged to deepen their academic knowledge). In the case of practice, the improvement was to come simply by working with new age-ranges and in unfamiliar subject areas.

As a tutor in the English department at Hereford College of Education in the late 1960s, I was, for example, allowed on request several blocks of half a day per week per term for this purpose. The choice of age and subject was left entirely to me, as was the responsibility of negotiating entry to the school and classroom. Indeed, I am still in touch with those colleagues in Hereford schools. From them I learnt a great deal. I have to admit, however, that on none of these occasions did I discuss with the teachers the deeper issues related to learning to teach and helping others to learn.

This was even true when I first worked with an entire class of third-year juniors in the early 1970s with the class teacher and 12 students all in one room. The project was entirely mine (many of my colleagues expressed deep reservations about it), and, certainly at the beginning, the teacher rather tagged along. (In fact, this project was the hesitant beginnings of the Double Focus strategy of school experience (see Chapter 10) which in 1981 I subsequently imported to London, in the face of new and initially dubious institute colleagues.)

In some respects, then, we have progressed from those earlier days. Now, lecturers (today called tutors) are much more ready and able to discuss issues and pedagogy and are more open about what theory can and cannot do. But unfortunately, because of the upheavel in schools in the 1980s, this has not come at an optimum time. Though ironically there is now compulsion on tutors to get into schools, this is actually less likely to involve new ground being covered, and indeed is being described in terms of 'refreshing their experience', which makes it sound like retreading old ground in order to update techniques and strategies. This is partly because in more difficult school conditions tutors are less disposed to take risks, and partly because compulsion does not motivate real exploration and experimentation.

The re-emergence of partnership

In the light of this background, then, it is more than somewhat ironic that in the later 1970s the goverment had taken up the notions to which the colleges were alert in the mid-1960s.

As the National Association of Teachers in Further and Higher Education (NATFHE) reminds us, the Secretary of State wrote, in 1970, to all universities acting as validating bodies asking them to review teacher education courses. The letter contained the following, as part of the list which, it claimed, public discussion had shown as subjects of concern:

> The organisation, supervision and assessment of teaching practice, and the role of the practising teacher in this field.

> The adequacy of the course in relation to practical teaching problems such as classroom organisation, the teaching of reading, backward learners . . . immigrant children and team education.

> The content and relevance of courses in the theory of education and the possibilities of developing educational concepts in a more practical manner and deferring some of the theoretical aspects to in-service education. (NATFHE, 1983, p.5)

These issues were picked up again by representatives of trainers in 1979, in a highly influential document to which the government documentation discussed below makes detailed reference.

The Universities Council for the Education and Training of Teachers (UCET) produced a transbinary consultative report written by Hirst on 'The PGCE Course and the Training of Specialist Teachers for Secondary Schools' in January 1979 (see Hirst, 1980). This report was concerned with courses in colleges and universities which were university validated. And it was secondary school oriented. Ironically, it was critical of the standards of supervision of teaching practice and its place in the training course. Yet, by contrast to the colleges' methods, the universities' approach to supervision had been traditionally less stringent, more impersonal, and less interested in the views of the class teachers. Further, supervision at secondary level is inevitably different in its mechanics from that at primary level. However, in spite of its specific focus, the critical flavour of this document became attached to teacher training in general and, as we shall see below, fuelled the government criticism and demands for improvement across the board. (See Fish, 1987.) Significantly, similar demands were also beginning to be made about schooling in a range of curriculum documents.

Let us now consider in detail the documents which, during the last 12 years since the beginning of the Great Debate, have been aimed at raising these issues about partnership.

The history of the rhetoric

Emerging concern about teacher training

The debates about the school curriculum, and standards of teacher training, have proceeded in parallel since Callaghan's Ruskin College speech of 1976. In both cases documents have emanated from both HMI and the DES, and in both cases the more recent HMI documents have become closer in tone and content to those of the DES.

Although neither *Primary Education in England* (HMSO 1978), nor *Aspects of Secondary Education in England* (HMSO, 1979), actually mention teacher training in detail, they nevertheless set the scene for concern about it. The inadequacies which caused particular horror in the primary and secondary HMI surveys were lack of qualification in the content areas by subject staff in secondary schools, and the lack of preparation for the range of curriculum areas to be covered by class teachers in the primary schools. Viewed coldly, it would seem somewhat ironic that these (indisputable) areas of problem should, after debate, lead to the vigorous promulgation of the idea that students should spend more time in school working with teachers.

Following *Primary Education in England* and *Aspects of Secondary Education in England*, and parallel with increasingly prescriptive documents on the school curriculum, there were, between 1981 and 1986, three HMI discussion papers, a White Paper, and two DES circulars, all of which made detailed reference to the notion of partnership in initial training. Most of these will be presented briefly in chronological order, as a means of providing teachers and students with the specific facts about the documentation, some of which, ironically, they are not normally in a position to see for themselves. Brief quotations from each document will serve to provide the flavour of the changing tone, the persistent content, and the rhetorical rather then philosophical nature of the statements about school-college partnership.

The first three publications to make major statements about Partnership were all HMI discussion papers, published by the DES. The two most important were: *Teacher Training in the Secondary School: The Implications of the HMI Survey*, published in January 1981; and *Teaching in Schools: The Content of Initial Training*, published in January 1983. Of these two documents, the second contains the more crystallised ideas and the more determined tone.

Teacher Training in the Secondary School

Talking of the final year of the BEd secondary honours course, this first document says:

> Students certainly need to be introduced to the language and thought of curriculum theory... They also need opportunities to look at a total school curriculum in action and to penetrate below the timetable and its analysis.
> This is a difficult task, but a start can be made by giving students opportunities of studying the curriculum in schools associated with the college. This reference to the practical is essential, for an attempt to introduce the view of the whole curriculum at a theoretical level, largely unrelated to practical experience of subject work, is not going to be effective. (DES, 1981, p.9)

Later, it continues:

> During school experience and block practice they are under pressure... to put into operation ideas they have met in lectures and tutorials, and there are the prevailing teaching styles of the school as a powerful influence in their own right... The aim is not to produce teachers with allegiance to a given approach to teaching, but with a repertoire of teaching styles... (DES, 1981, p.13)

These suggestions amount to little more than an exhortation to link practice with theory – though by applying it. There is, however, a lack of understanding here about how the colleges operate.

When it talks about the teaching practice as the occasion when students put into operation what they have been told in lectures, it reveals a traditional and product-oriented view of training. But the eminently reasonable tone of the document, which has turned out to be the most tentative of all of them, is captured in phrases suggesting that students should be 'given opportunities' to look at schools (the word 'opportunities' recurs), that colleges should be 'concerned' for the coordination of school-college links, and that the colleges' role is to 'allow' students to develop a range of skills. There is nothing here, then, that is prescriptive.

Teaching in Schools: The Content of Initial Training

Such a statement cannot be made, however, about the second of these papers. In the following extracts it becomes clear that by 1983 the tone has changed, as indeed it has in the school curriculum documents. The sentences here have become declamatory, and falling cadences are much in evidence, indicating that this is a laying down of the law. For example, the tone of the following brooks no argument:

> The professional skills which initial training can give to an intending teacher lie at the heart of the training process. School experience and teaching practice are the firm basis for professional training, since it is in the observation of skilled teachers, in the practice of his own teaching in partnership with such teachers, in sharing their planning and discussing how their work is organised, that a student can help develop the skills which his studies have enabled him to identify and analyse. (DES, 1983a, p.10)

There are some worrying issues here. It is to be hoped that it is merely rather self-conscious phrasing in the first sentence, and not a belief that this is what training is about, which leads to the suggestion that professional skills are 'given' to the students by initial training. But by the end of the second sentence it does begin to seem that the view of this paper is that 'skills' are seen as the central and major content of the training. Finally, the false dichotomy implicit in the second sentence completes the impression that the writers of the paper are clinging to an archaic model of teacher training. The suggestion is that on teaching practice and school experience students develop skills which they have heard about and already analysed in college. Yet this analysis is the very point of the school experience work. There seems here to be much vagueness about what can profitably be learnt by students in schools as opposed to in college.

The paper continues by using the recommendation of the UCET report, presumably in an attempt to indicate that these ideas are not being imposed from outside the training sector.

> The partnership between initial training institutions and schools should be strengthened in the ways recommended by the UCET transbinary consultative report of January 1979 on *The PGCE Course and the Training of Specialist Teachers in Secondary Schools* which include:
>
> > 'Tutors and (school) teachers collaborating closely on the criteria and procedures for selecting students on the course;
> >
> > The staff of training institutions and those staff of the schools responsible for the day-to-day work of training, teaching in each other's institutions . . .
> >
> > Members of staff of both institutions together taking part in work with students both in schools and in the training institutions.'

The paper continues to quote:

> 'experimenting with carefully considered schedules of assessment for practical teaching across a wide range of activities.' (DES, 1983a, pp.10–11)

Having made the point that these ideas had come initially from the training sector, but omitting the point that these words were not originally applied to all of it, the paper continues rather testily:

> Recommendations of this kind have been made for many years, and some institutions follow the practices discussed. If a true partnership is to be effected with the teaching profession, such examples of good practice should extend to all initial training courses. (DES, 1983a, p.11)

Here, at last then, the gauntlet had been laid down. The above recommendations by UCET were ways of exploring and improving teacher training. But as this HMI discussion paper implies, these ideas were about to be taken at face value and hardened up as compulsory elements of the training institution's profile. In this new form, their coercive nature somehow simplifies and distorts the original ideas.

The UCET recommendations, then, were to become the new measures of quality in a battle to improve both teaching and training, in a set of government moves, emanating from the DES, to centralise control over the training curriculum as well as the school curriculum. In order to make the new rules clear, within three months of the appearance of HMI's *Teaching in Schools*, the White Paper, *Teaching Quality*, was published by HMSO. This organised the machinery for taking control of these matters. Within 15 months of the White Paper, the Secretary of State had issued *Circular 3/84* (DES, 1984) which clearly set out his demarcation lines. Both documents indicated the rules by which courses of training must run, or must cease to exist. These, then, were no longer matters of discussion fuelled by HMI. Equally, they appear not to have been matters of extensive educational debate at governmental level.

The machinery for partnership

Teaching Quality

Teaching Quality, which appeared in March 1983, announced that the Secretary of State (finding new and somewhat arbitrary powers) would establish local and national control bodies and criteria for a new form of approval for initial training courses, in consultation with professional bodies. The framework for the new mode of approval, and the broad categories for the criteria, were described as relating to both professional and academic content of courses, and to good working relations with schools. The framework would enable training institutions and professional committees to plan and scrutinise courses before submitting them to Secretaries of State for approval. This accreditation procedure would be applied to all courses throughout England and Wales, irrespective of the maturity of the course itself. The initial statement requires that:

> the initial teacher training of all qualified teachers should include studies closely linked with practical experience in school, and involving the active participation of experienced practising schoolteachers. (HMSO, 1983, para 64, p.19)

In itself, of course, this was thoroughly unexceptionable. Its significance in the

Secretary of State's eyes, and therefore for the colleges, appeared in the paragraph immediately following.

> The Government believe that these requirements can only be met if the teaching staff in the training institutions are themselves equipped to educate and train the entrants to an all graduate profession. In addition, in order to satisfy the third requirement, a sufficient proportion to each training institution's staff should have enjoyed success as teachers in schools, and their school experience should be recent, substantial and relevant. Many of the staff do not now have such experience. Those staff who are concerned with pedagogy should also have continuing regular contact with classroom teaching ... The establishment of close links between training establishments and suitable schools in their vicinity will facilitate arrangements along these lines. (HMSO, 1983, para 65, pp.19–20)

The issues begged here and which were inevitably shut out of the debate in the Secretary of State's attempt to produce simple *measures* of quality were those about how tutors might best be 'equipped' to foster learning through practice, and those about the relationship between practical experience and the ability to facilitate that practice in others.

Circular 3/84

By the time *Circular 3/84* had arrived in the training institutions, therefore, it had little to do but to reinforce these comments and turn them into an assortment of hurdles to be jumped. Accordingly, the Circular itself simply announced the Secretary of State's conclusions on the machinery through which he was prepared to say that the course was suitable for the professional preparation of teachers and would lead to the conferment upon students of teacher status. It transpired that the machinery was to be vested in a newly established Council for the Accreditation of Teacher Education, and that this Council was to advise on approval for both the state and the university sectors of teacher education. It was in the annex to the Circular that the vital measures of the suitability of teacher-training courses to produce a quality product were to be found.

Five of the 17 criteria which must be met before a course is approved to run relate to the school/college relationship. The first two criteria relate generally to course approval. There then follow clauses about links between training institutions and schools, thus:

> 3. Institutions, in cooperation with local authoritites and their advisers, should establish links with a number and variety of schools, in the surrounding area, and courses should be developed and run in close working partnership with those schools. Experienced teachers from schools should assume joint responsibility with the training institutions for the planning and supervision of students' school experience and teaching practice and should take a major role in the assessment of students' practical performance ...
>
> 4. ... the staff concerned with pedagogy should have school teaching experience. They should have enjoyed recent success as teachers ... (of the age-range to which

their training courses are directed), and should maintain regular and frequent experience of classroom teaching . . .

5. Initial teacher-training courses should be so planned as to allow for a substantial element of school experience and teaching practice . . . Educational and professional studies should be closely linked with each other and with a student's practical experience in schools. (DES, 1984, annex)

It is perhaps as well to pause here in order to disentangle the factual issues from the assumptions. There would seem to be at least the following four kinds of assumption in the above criteria:

1. The partnership in planning, teaching and supervising the initial training course assumes on the part of teachers the motivation, the ability, the time, and the resources to do so.
2. It is assumed that by virtue of their classroom teaching experience in schools, teachers are equipped, willing, and able to plan, supervise, support, and assess students, and contribute to their college-based work, without either induction to this work, or in-service support for it.
3. It is assumed that regular experience of teaching in a school classroom is an essential precursor and the only precursor to facilitating students' learning of these skills.
4. The myth of the natural goodness of practice is perpetuated in the idea that the length of practice automatically affects and improves the quality of it.

But there are further requirements in the Circular also. Later, under the heading of Educational and Professional Studies, it emerges, in clause 10, that students should be provided with 'adequate mastery' of basic teaching skills. It also seems in this clause, from demands about the extent of school experience, that the Secretary of State wants quantity yet again to be his reassurance about quality. This has echoes of attitudes found in documents about the school curriculum. Yet it is not how much intermittent experience the course provides *in relation to* teaching practice that will affect standards, but how much more precisely the training procedures can be related to the training intention. In order to improve these matters, what we actually need is a better idea of what various of the training procedures available can best achieve. Parts 2 and 3 of this book deal with this question.

CATENOTE 4

Having set out the requirements for approval of training courses, it remained for the DES to offer the partners some clarification and support. Accordingly, in January 1986, a new Circular, *CATENOTE 4*, arrived in the training institutions from Elizabeth House. Its heading, 'Links Between Initial Training Institutions and Schools', indicates its significance. It is ironic, therefore, that it was not also distributed to schools. Apparently the purpose of the Catenote is to 'offer some guidance as to how the relevant criteria might be met'. Basically it seeks to draw attention to three interlinked issues in which school/college links operate most directly. These are:

> the organisation, management and assessment of students' teaching practice and school experience; the involvement of schoolteachers in the selection and training of students within institutions; and the provision of opportunities for the staff of training institutions, particularly those concerned with pedagogy, to demonstrate and re-inforce their own teaching effectiveness in schools. (DES, 1986, para 4, p.3)

It is worth noticing here that the assessment of teaching practice has been formally attached to the planning and management of it, and made the responsibility of joint partnership. By contrast, it is significant that the third aspect refers only to tutors rather than to a teacher/tutor exchange, and that the words used here are: 'demonstrate', which suggests giving public proof; 're-inforce', which implies that in some undefined way automatic weakness in teaching skills and techniques is related directly to time intervals between periods of practice; and 'effectiveness' (the measure of which is highly problematic). It might well, in at least some cases, be a good thing for tutors to return to classroom teaching, but (for some at least) the reasons might be quite other than to prove effectiveness.

But there is more to come. Clause 5 contains the idea that in school students should develop and test the practical classroom skills to which they had been introduced elsewhere in the course. Tutors are told that they should share in the experience of day-to-day classroom practice by teaching in front of and alongside the students, and schools are told that they can make a significant contribution to the preparation of future members of the profession. Here, too, we still have the notion that skills are 'taught' on the college course, and are then 'applied' in schools.

Clause 15 takes up issues about assessment, indicating that some heads and teachers have agreed to act as student assessors. This complements the judgements of tutors and schools on the quality of each student's performance, which is finally agreed by consultation between assessors, teachers and tutors, But this seriously underrates the shift of thinking actually necessary for many teachers to be prepared to take part in a process which can involve failing students. Evidence emerged, in a small survey conducted in 1986 across two London boroughs, that of 50 staff interviewed, 22 were unhappy about the idea of teachers' direct involvement in deciding the students' fate on teaching practice.

The Circular continues:

> 16. The examples of co-operative working outlined above provide some useful ways of ensuring that teacher trainers and practising teachers understand each others' aims and purposes.
> What they have in common is a spirit of partnership through which both trainers and teachers can make their own contributions towards a shared professional objective. (DES, 1986, p. 7)

This is more encouraging. What is needed is energy to be spent in trying to elucidate in more detail how these two partners can refine their own complementary skills and expertise for the improvement of the training process. For this, we need to learn more about the process involved in learning through practice and exactly how it can be better fostered.

The life of CATE

Interestingly, the tone of *CATENOTE 4* suggests a national body that is indisputably and powerfully in charge of teacher training, and which has vast experience of this responsibility. Yet, of course, it was set up in 1984 by Sir Keith Joseph. Though equipped with impressive teeth, it has not found favour everywhere. For example, *The Third Report of the House of Commons Committee on Education, Science and the Arts* (HMSO, 1987) makes it quite clear that the select committee 'do not favour the continuation of CATE after its initial term of appointment expires' (HMSO, 1987, para 12.75, p.ccviii).

Indeed, this machinery comes to an end in 1989, but having provided the Secretary of State for Education with such a useful control mechanism, is now due to be replaced by other powers. Before its demise, it will have worked its way through all the initial teacher-training courses in every institution in the country, applying to each the above criteria and others not here recorded because they are not directly relevant to this chapter.

All course proposals submitted to CATE must first have been considered by the local version of this machinery (local CATE). Such committees, set up by each training institution, consist of local teachers, LEA advisers and representatives of local industry. It is here, with local CATE, that many of the difficulties of the whole system have been revealed. Broadly the problems, which have emerged throughout the country, include the following:

- the lack of time and knowledge on the part of teachers and industrial representatives to scrutinise proposals
- lack of incentive to attend on the part of LEA personnel in the light of present high demands on their role
- lack of a clear constituency for those teacher representatives who may be committing colleagues to all sorts of new responsibilities in agreeing to new courses, but who have no mandate for this and no direct means of reporting matters to them
- a range of problems implicit in the fact that the committees were set up by the colleges and are often not chaired by neutral parties.

It is unfortunate that the will to overcome these problems stemmed from negative rather than positive forces in that it emerged from the colleges' need to obtain committee support for accreditation of courses, rather than from the committees' belief in the idea of partnership. But, with the advent of more recent initiatives, it may well prove to be more than unfortunate.

Latest initiatives

With the publication by the DES of the Green Paper, *Qualified Teacher Status*, in May 1988 (DES, 1988a) and subsequent government initiatives, there is now a major move to license graduates as unqualified teachers and to offer them training only after they are employed, and to make all initial training school-based. Thus, the way is being opened up to aspiring teachers to learn on the job, with what could be minimum induction and training. Once again the administrative arguments predominate. Such a move will, it is being argued: meet the current teacher shortage; prepare the way for a freer movement of graduates within the European Economic Community in 1992; save money on those considerable numbers who train but do not (immediately) enter teaching; and please all those who harbour doubts about teacher training. Behind such arguments come the educational ones about keeping in line with new ideas of learning from practice and the (as yet unproven) success of school-based training courses. It is unfortunate that these educational arguments are based upon a simplistic view of learning to teach and learning from practice. It is significant that among all these arguments less is being said about the implications for those practising qualified professionals now in school who are likely to bear the brunt of this work.

The machinery for school/college partnership in teacher training was set up summarily in the early 1980s. But in reality on training courses throughout most of the 1980s there has been much successful work in respect of the practice of partnership. (See Chapter 1 and Chapters 7 to 10.) It would seem a wilful waste of the knowledge and experience gained if the latest teacher-training initiatives ignored the fruits of this or its future potential.

Whatever the actual machinery for training new teachers, for the process to be a success it must be rooted in deep understandings of *both* the realities of professional practice *and* a reconceptualisation of theory. The following four chapters focus upon these issues. They indicate that such understandings are by no means an automatic result of simply being placed in a practical setting.

3. Professional Perspectives Now: Partnership in a Complex World

Summary

- The present context for learning to teach
  - the professional in a changing world
  - the nature of present practice
  - the demands on schooling
  - tensions related to schooling
  - the usefulness of untidiness and uncertainty
- Learning professional practice now
  - what sort of practitioners are needed now?
  - what should be the nature of their training?
  - what might be learnt in the practical setting?
- Some implications for staff and schools
  - demands upon the school
  - new demands upon qualified teachers
  - the role of teacher as trainer

Introduction

The intention of this chapter is threefold. First, it seeks to recognise and to take stock of the school context in which much of teacher training is presently, and will continue to be, carried out. That is, it seeks as realistic a view as possible of the whole (inevitably untidy) practical arena. Second, it considers in general what is involved in learning professional practice now. Third, and in the light of these two, it seeks to look at some of the implications of involvement with initial training for the staff and school.

The present context for learning to teach

The professional in a changing world

Like all professions, teaching has in recent years experienced enormous upheaval. Schön (1983) has pointed out that the professions are now essential to society and are responsible for the conduct of much of society's business, and that the position of the professional has been coveted for both its accompanying status and monetary rewards. However, alongside (or because of) this increased dependence by society upon the professions and an increased reaction against authority, there are now signs of nervousness and doubt about the behaviour and status of the professions and professionals generally. This has, in part at least, been brought about by some professionals' misuse of autonomy.

In the past, the closed and separate identity of the professional group with its specialist knowledge and skill meant that the responsibility for the profession's conduct and ethics was vested in the whole profession and each individual within it. Thus, because of assumptions about their exclusivity and expertise, professionals were granted autonomy by the community they served. With the advent of the consumer society, there has been a major call for accountability, which requires the professional to submit both his conduct and his actions to public scrutiny. Currently this has led to calls for the public evaluation of courses of training within the professions, and to the appraisal of professional *performance*. The public now claim their own right to judge the processes as well as the products of the original performance and its appraisal. For these reasons, the lines between the professional's knowledge, rights, responsibilities and status and those of the public are becoming blurred.

One result of this in the teaching profession is the call to partnership in the running of schools by local governors in conjunction with heads and staff; another is the involvement of parents in the school classroom; a third is the move to divide professional training between the practitioners and the trainers.

A major result is the urgent need for professionals to be able to explicate their actions in terms of the theories that inform them, and to be able to compare these with alternative theories.

The signs of these changes are everywhere. Examples can be cited within and across occupations. They include the following:

- the reaction of parents, governors, LEAs and government to the William Tyndale affair (where parents were in conflict with school staff over the running of the school)
- the suing of doctors for negligence or for mistakes or for activities associated with private gain
- the apparent disintegration of professional knowledge, and the loss of faith in professional judgement as a result of conflicting advice being given by different professionals
- the professional pluralism which now encourages the advertising of a wide range of values, beliefs and practices within one profession
- the questioning of the whole position and status of professionals and their associated 'middle-class' image
- the evident overloading of professionals in terms of work, which calls in doubt their ability to cope, to organise or to maintain high standards, and which is unpopular in an age of unemployment
- the fluctuating fortunes of whole professions and the changing patterns of demand upon them, which have rendered many professionals

redundant
- the problem of maintaining the relevance of what professionals know and do in such rapidly changing times
- the consequent inadequacy of professional knowledge to address some of the problems of society
- the apparent failure of theory to relate to and enlighten practice
- the apparent irrelevance of some aspects of training in some professions and the slowness to change training programmes
- the pressures of management towards efficiency, delivery and performance in spite of the problematic nature of professional practice.

If this is the general context in which teachers must train, then present practice in schools further reflects this.

The nature of present practice

A chief characteristic of present practice in schools is an inevitable untidiness. The nature of this untidiness, which emanates from the continual attempt to refine and improve professional practice, is perhaps best captured in this quotation from a speech by Anne Jones:

> In the recent HMI inspection of my school by a team of 29 delightful and highly intelligent HMI, I was constantly caught in a tension between the traditional and the transitional. There was a sense in which they seemed to be counting caterpillar legs, whereas we were trying to produce something quite different, namely butterflies. Furthermore, they caught us at the chrysalis stage, when it was rather difficult to judge what would eventually come out the other end. We found ourselves backtracking in order to produce evidence of caterpillar legs. However, in my view our caterpillar legs were not very convincing because we were in the process of giving them up and moving on to a new way of working. So there was a built-in tension or dissonance between what we were actually trying to do, and what we thought we were expected to have done. (Jones, 1985, p.453)

This graphic imagery of a caterpillar and butterfly vividly gives the flavour of what students and tutors will always find in any school placement in which the student seeks practical experience. This is because schools and schooling are, and should be, eternally evolving.

This state of affairs, though potentially embarrassing to the visited practitioners, is in fact extremely helpful to the process of training. But it is only likely to be helpful if all those involved in the training process (that is, teachers, tutors, and students) seek to understand better both why this evolving process exists and how it can be used in training. Such a seeking of knowledge is best carried out in practice, but the reflection upon it and deliberation about it arguably need a more distanced arena.

Practising and thinking about practice in a context which is in the process of change is helpful for trainees in ensuring that their training is relevant and flexible, and for the qualified teacher in seeing that practice from a new perspective. Students enter practice not as public visitors or prospective clients, for whom it may be important to provide a tidy, efficient image of the school, but as serious seekers after knowledge of how things really are.

The demands on schooling

Probably the greatest number of simultaneous demands in history are currently being made on Britain's schools, primary and secondary. Very extensive changes have been set in motion by the 1988 Education Reform Act. These join the demands of new examinations, profiling, and the need for new teaching strategies in the secondary school. There are new expectations from industry and the world of work, new arrangements for pupils with special needs, for policies towards anti-racism, anti-sexism, for equal opportunities, for micro-technology, and for teaching about AIDS. There are the new approaches to the governing of schools and to the sharing of the responsibilities for decisions about the curriculum. There are increasing difficulties in respect of discipline and control as the policies of previous years are coming home to roost. There is the backlog of results of several years of teachers' action, and a new ethos brought about by Directed Time. (Directed Time is the term commonly used in schools to denote the 195 days and 1265 hours which teachers must now work in each 12 month period from 1 September. During this time they must perform duties specified by the head teacher (DES, 1987, p.25).) Among these pressures new teachers are having to be trained in schools, partnership in training is being forged between the training institutions and schools, and students are having to learn both how to adapt to present circumstances and how to stay flexible enough to adapt to forthcoming further changes. This inevitably leads to tensions, which need to be shared openly by the partners in training.

Tensions related to schooling

Many tensions arise from conflicting ideas about schooling, and uncertainties about newer approaches to teaching and learning. Among others these may be characterised as:

- pupils' dependence on teachers versus their autonomy as learners
- active versus passive modes of learning
- the pressures of parental expectations of involvement in the classroom versus less parental support for schooling
- pressure for the teacher to be both expert and widely knowledgeable
- emphasis on the processes of learning versus the expectations about end-products
- issues about rights versus issues about responsibilities of all those involved with schools
- the empowering of pupils as masters of their own learning versus the authority of the teacher as expert
- the emphasis upon, versus an attempt to ignore, the ideological and political dimensions of education

- the demand for classrooms to be more publicly open versus the need to protect children
- the pupils' and teachers' ability to make decisions and judgements versus a blind acceptance of those made by other people
- cooperative learning versus competitive learning
- the view of teaching as interacting exclusively with children versus the view that it should involve appraisal and evaluation
- the conflicting requirements of a pluralist society
- the questioning of the value of academic achievement and individual success versus the importance of 'coping, caring and cooperation'
- the teacher as a manager of learning rather than an imparter of information
- learning by discovery and principle rather than by rote and rule
- the blurring of the barriers between school and the outside world versus the isolationist approach of some schools
- the undervaluing of the status of a teacher in society (as seen in the pay disputes), together with the erosion of the notion of authority itself, and the failure of teachers as yet to redefine their role in the light of the revolutionary changes in society
- the need for considerable changes to be faced without additional resources in an increasingly diminishing budget.

The issue that underlies most of these tensions is that of a mismatch between the educational aims of schooling and the utilitarian requirements of society. And it has cashed out into a formidable list of specific conflicts. Yet, ironically, while society is happy to place schools under these pressures, it does not yet happily tolerate the accompanying upheaval that this brings with it. The 1988 Education Reform Act seeks to simplify and streamline what schools offer into a National Curriculum which resolves these conflicts by statute, removing all effective argument and even controlling future experimentation. But the Act cannot control the tide of human nature, creativity and adaptation, and wisely it does not seek to impose methodology. Such tensions, then, will – even should – remain.

The usefulness of untidiness and uncertainty

Schools, then, demonstrate daily the conflicts of ideology and priorities which must be expected of a human institution in the present pluralist, post-industrial society. And they will contine to do so. But such contradictions and conflicts can be the basis for a training which provokes the trainee to challenge her own perceptions about education.

The important element in all this is the confidence with which these contradictions, problems and uncertainties are handled by the school and the college, the teacher and the trainer, and what they teach the student.

Learning professional practice now

Views about what a student should learn *through* practice are dependent upon views about what is involved in the activity of teaching and learning, and how theory and practice are regarded. These issues are all taken up in detail in Chapter 4. The following three questions can be considered here, however:

1. Given the untidy and unpredictable nature of professional practice, what sort of practitioner should the training course attempt to provide? That is, what should be the goal of initial training?
2. What kind of training course does this necessitate? That is, what should be the nature of training?
3. What can be learnt in a practical setting?

What sort of practitioners are needed now?

Given the speed of change in society and the professions at present, and the demand for teachers to adapt to these, what is needed in the last decade of the twentieth century are teachers who can think on their feet, and learn from and during this process; who can create new personal theory rather than being dependent on previously learnt routines; and who can work from first principles to design, use and then evaluate new approaches to teaching. And that design process needs to take account not only of the means but also the ends of education, so as to safeguard the moral dimensions of what is done in its name, and so that the professionals can bear their part in the inevitable public debates about education. It is for these reasons that what is argued for in this book is that training courses should seek to produce reflective and deliberative practitioners.

Given the rapidly changing nature of education and society and the need to fuel that deliberation and reflection and debate with systematically uncovered and professionally weighed evidence, the training course ought also to produce a practitioner who can enquire into his own practice, and be articulate about the enquiry processes, the evidence and the conclusions to which they lead.

Further, given the introduction of open learning and life-long education, and the developments in data management with their consequent slackening of emphasis on memory and data manipulation, broadly what is now needed are teachers with a wide range of skills and strategies for facilitating learning.

What should be the nature of their training?

Given the above goals, there follow many issues about the means of educating such reflective, deliberative and enquiry-based enablers of learning. These are considered in detail in Chapter 6. The following questions are designed to raise some of the most important ones:

1. *What should be the scope of the training course?* Should it offer a broad

perspective on the profession, which enables students from the beginning to locate their work as teachers in an appropriate theoretical framework, should it offer radical alternatives to education, schooling and society, or should it focus on a narrower set of skills?
2. *What should be the orientation of the training course?* Should it be school-focused, that is, concerned to provide a means of adapting to a specific set of practical and parochial problems as a means of survival, and as a means of focusing on real problems, leaving wider issues until later in the career? Or should wider perspectives be offered from the beginning? (This question is particularly crucial for the course which is entirely school-based, or when the licensed teacher is learning on the job.)
3. *Should the course illustrate or avoid the complexities of both content and methods in initial training?* Is the knowledge base of teaching itself to be regarded as given and static, or changing and to be enquired into? Should the course separate the personal from the professional education of the student, and if so, which should be emphasised?
4. *What should be the course's attitudes to the nature of the school system?* Given the 1988 Education Reform Act, to what extent is present school practice able to be changed and to what extent should students be prepared to question what is required of them? Should students accept the agenda set by the trainers and the education system, contribute to it, change it, and/or learn about themselves?
5. *What should be the role of theory and practice?* What is theory? Should theory be integrated with, linked to, or differentiated from practice? Which theoretical aspects should be emphasised? How can the student learn, and be helped to learn through practice? How can the trainers foster such learning?
6. *Are the students there to learn their own styles or be initiated into those of others?* Does the training goal of producing reflective and deliberative practitioners allow enough for individual differences? Should the student learn about herself as well as about teaching?

Beneath these questions lies the issue about what can be learnt in practice.

What might be learnt in the practical setting?

This question has just become particularly apposite. Again it has to be said that there is no natural goodness in practice. What matters is the *provision made* for the student to learn from and through practice. Among other things this provision ought to include opportunities to learn the processes of reflection, deliberation and enquiry, to experiment, to make and learn from mistakes, and to formulate personal theory. It ought to involve the provision of time to reflect and deliberate, the opportunity to do so away from the practical arena, and disinterested help with these processes. Such provision might be able to be offered by one, rather than both of the present partners in training, if that person were able to combine all of the knowledge, skills, capacities, and experience of the teacher and the tutor. It seems hard, however, to see how the licensed teacher approach could allow for the kind of joint deliberations on a shared practical experience, as described in Chapters 7 to 10.

Schön (1987b) and Cameron-Jones (1987) have argued for a practicum, a sheltered arena in which the student can learn some of these complex processes without taking full responsibility for the class. It is this aspect of training, sometimes meant by the term 'intermittent experience', which is beginning to provide some useful work both in training and in the investigation of training. It would be a retrograde step in many ways were this work to cease.

Given, then, the demands of present professional practice and the present and near future approaches to training, what are the implications of training for the schools?

Some implications for staff and schools

Demands upon the school

The enterprise of training the teacher, once taken on board, cannot but be a whole-school matter. For one thing, the trainee is never confined to a corner, and often, like pupils, will learn from the hidden curriculum a range of things that are far from intended.

Account, too, needs to be taken of the differences and distinctions between the priorities of the practical situation and the needs of training. And there needs to be a whole staff commitment to seeing training as an ever ongoing part of all the daily priorities and processes of the school. Thus, for the sake of both experienced professionals and trainees, ways have to be found in schools of locating the training priority in the crowded weather chart of all the pressures of work in school.

In the light of all this, it seems somewhat ironic that it is now, when schools are perhaps most stretched in terms of demands versus resources, that the government has chosen to place teacher training even more firmly on the shoulders of teachers.

It is somewhat disappointing that none of these matters has figured in the Grant-Related In-service Training (GRIST) priorities at either government or local authority level as yet. This, of course, also depends on the high profile nature of the training enterprise within an authority, or a school, and this in turn will be partly the result of how importantly the case is pleaded for training and for various techniques within that training. For the training institutions and for the future of training itself it is essential to keep these debates in the forefront of the minds of colleagues in schools.

Certainly there are many who believe that only by establishing a contractual agreement with the school will teacher training be properly placed on the school's agenda. Such views have not until recently, however, included the idea of basing all training in the school. This notion brings with it the need to consider the reciprocal rights and responsibilities of the school and the student (or unqualified teacher) in training.

New demands upon qualified teachers

All of the above issues demand not only that current professional practitioners in school are able to give an account of and explain to the public the complexities of their own situation. It also means that they are required to take responsibility for the training of entrants to the profession in these matters.

This all requires the practitioner to be, in Hoyle's terms, an extended professional (Hoyle, 1974). Among other things, it means that the professional needs to be able to:

- accept and understand the need for a constant reconsideration of practice and theory, that is, be a constantly reflective (self-appraising) practitioner
- give an account of and articulate the basis of practice
- expound on the difficulties of a range of issues about training, including the complexities of theory and practice
- respond to the call for appraisal within an understanding of the problematic nature of that notion
- see his own practice within a wider context
- be able concomitantly to foster learning and learn to foster it; to demonstrate that process personally, to encourage it in colleagues, and to facilitate it in trainees.

These demands are considerable. Yet there is, as yet, little direct training or support for those trying to respond to them.

The role of teacher as trainer

The role of teacher as trainer is a complex one and involves special expertise in addition to that associated with teaching. Much of the practical work described in Parts 2 and 3 provides detailed perspectives upon this. The key point to be made at this stage is that 'having a student', or having responsibility for a licensed teacher, makes additional demands, and these cannot easily be quantified even at an individual level. A commitment to what the training procedures are intended to achieve is important, together with the willingness and ability to see the ongoing problems and issues of the classroom as fruitful material for learning for both teacher and trainee as well as pupils. This actually takes considerable confidence, and a major commitment to the processes of training, as well as expertise in working with students in ways which are designed to facilitate their learning to teach. Arguably, such ways should be informed by up-to-date knowledge of work in this rapidly developing field.

Even among those teachers who by everyone's standards are the most successful in the classroom, there might exist many for whom training others is neither a preference nor a strength. The concert pianist is not necessarily the best teacher of piano; the top-class athlete is not always the best coach. And one of the distinctions arises from the contrast between the drive to perfect one's own performance and the vocation to facilitate that of others.

To admit this distinction, however, is to accept that there might be different expertise in teaching itself and in training others to teach. Such an admission, of course, brings with it the notions that teachers and trainers might well have different priorities within a training programme as well as in their agendas for schooling itself. But such an admission also points up the very positive advantages to the student of both perspectives. For this reason, it is a pity that the government has placed its emphasis on the similarities between teachers and trainers, as if the credibility of the trainers rests on their ability as teachers (see Chapter 2), and as if any successful teacher in school will automatically be both willing and able to take responsibility for the trainee.

Some, of course, might. But they will need to combine a fairly formidable list of knowledge, skills, capacities, and dispositions if they are to offer the best of both the teacher's and the tutor's contribution to training. They would also need to keep in mind an important distinction between their work with pupils and that with students. Whatever a pupil's weaknesses, a teacher must endeavour to make the best of him and to help him make the best of himself. Whereas, in professional training, if trainees do not show aptitude, if their stengths do not lie in working with pupils, if they prove incapable of fostering learning in others, they must not be retained on the training course.

Calling for such distinctions between teaching and training to be clarified, however, is not the same as calling for the reinforcement of earlier notions of the separation of theory and practice, as the following chapter will show.

4. Theory and Practice Now: The Context for Initial Training

Summary

- Theory and practice now: towards some crucial distinctions
  - practice, action and praxis
  - theory
  - theory out of practice
  - the gap, real or unreal?
  - the problematic nature of theory and practice
- Some present dilemmas about professional practice
  - what kind of activity is teaching?
  - what kind of activity is learning?
  - what theory do teachers need to know?
- Five views of theory and practice
  - the intuitive view
  - the common-sense view
  - the applicatory view
  - the creative view
  - the reconstructionist view
  - some comments

Introduction

There has been, and to some extent still is, at large in the teaching profession, and among qualified practitioners in other professions, a deep-seated and very considerable reaction against the whole idea of Theory. It is still (quite wrongly) associated in the minds of many with college-based and largely irrelevant study of the foundation disciplines of Education (the history, philosophy, psychology and sociology of education). As such, it is seen as existing at the far side of an unbridgeable void from practice. Part of the reason for all of this is that a large majority of the present members of the professions were trained at a time when theory was conceived of as of this kind. While they are fully aware of the enormous changes elsewhere in education in the last ten years, they have not been made aware of the equally extensive changes in the thinking about theory and its relationship to practice in the training institutions. They have not been made privy to those new views of theory which place the practitioner at the heart of theory and turn research into the handmaid rather than the frustrated taskmaster of practice.

Of course, over the years, many theorists have believed in and fuelled notions of the elitism of theory and theorists, and of the separateness of theory from practice. Further, the very deployment of practitioners and trainers-of-practitioners respectively in schools on the one hand, and colleges or universities on the other, has institutionalised this dichotomy. And, too, there is still no consensus among academics about what theory is, about what it can offer, and about its relationship to practice.

At another level, however, if the government is attempting to nudge schools towards greater involvement in teacher training, and if other professions are to come to terms with the new demands upon them from differently structured training courses, there is clearly an enormous need for much groundwork to be done, and much discussion to be undertaken in this area. At a minimum it seems reasonable to suggest that this should include ensuring that *all* those involved in professional training are aware of the whole range of possible meanings of, and approaches to, theory and are alert to all the possible ways in which it can facilitate the improvement of practice.

Perhaps the most important change in the role of theory for professional practitioners has been called to our attention by Schön (1983). He points out that our idea of theory as something to be *applied* to practice arose because of our limited model of theory and practice which has been inappropriately derived from strictly scientific activities. He draws attention to the fact that since all professional practice is complex, unique and unpredictable because it deals with people, and because of the 'irreducible element of art' in it, theory can be seen to have an essentially more complex relationship with practice. Thus, the practitioner's personal theories of action need to be teased out by means of careful reflection on practice. (See Schön, 1983, p.18.) This state of affairs has serious and extensive implications for the training of practitioners. It also requires practising professionals to have clear ideas about the nature of the activities in which they engage. For this reason it is important to clarify some ideas about theory and its relationship to practice. In doing so we should remember that this is a complex and evolving field.

Theory and practice now: towards some crucial distinctions

Practice, action and praxis

When we talk about practical activities, that is, activities in which action is involved, we might be talking about complex activities like teaching or more apparently simple actions like cleaning a bicycle. In either case (the complex or the relatively more simple activity), we might easily carry out the actions or practices associated with it in one of three ways:

1. at all points blindly, following whim, fancy and chance (that is, if such vacancy of mind ever exists, without any sense at all)

2. in an instinctive way, that is, uncritically, following the actions as we always have, and guided only by habit, custom or ritual (that is, rationally but unreflectively)
3. by thinking about how we are doing now and, perhaps, how we have done this activity last time, in order to learn from the experience and make it, in some way, more efficient and/or effective (that is, reflectively).

(Clearly the first two above could be changed into the third version by the application of critical thought.)

In all of these cases, either the word 'action' or 'practice' could be applied, yet neither word makes clear whether the activity is done rationally but unreflectively, irrationally, or reflectively with a view to improvement.

Clearly, however, if there is to be any systematic improvement in the action or practice, there must be some sort of critical thought about the activity, and at best this might be before, during and after the activity. The task of such critical thought must be to act as what Eisner would call 'midwife', to bring to life and examine what operates beneath the surface of thought and activity (Eisner, 1985).

Thus the process of thought/reflection will facilitate the examination of the instinct/intuition, aid the conscious salvaging of the most useful and perhaps generalisable aspects of the activity and the rejection of the least useful, and turn instinct and intuition (and even whim and chance) into insight.

This kind of 'critical' activity might best be charaterised as reflection. Its processes need to be systematic and some of them are described in detail in Chapter 5. In order to indicate that the action or practice in which we are involved has this kind of character, then, we would have to call it 'reflective practice'. It is at this point that those familiar with Aristotelian thought will remember that the Greeks had one word for this – *praxis*. Carr and Kemmis (1986) provide a detailed review of Aristotle's ideas.

It is when we look at praxis in context, then, that we realise just how much this thinking about practice can actually encompass. It is concerned with reflecting upon the character and consequences of action, the conditions which determine it, and the knowledge which informs it. And in all of this there is concern for the moral dimension – a concern for ends as well as means, for what ought to be as well as what is. This we might call 'deliberation'. Thus, we also begin to see that the process of this kind of reflection and deliberation involves drawing upon a vast range of insights from a range of disciplines and that it also involves producing theory or theorising about practice. This leads us to the next question: what, then, is theory?

Theory

Theory might be defined, to start with, as a speculative system of ideas put forward in explanation of what has been, is, or might be.

In the past, traditional ideas about Education Theory saw it as that drawn from the so-called foundation disciplines of Education (philosophy, psychology, history, and sociology). More recently, other disciplines, like linguistics, politics, economics, and law, have also been seen to offer useful perspectives. Some cross-disciplinary studies, like educational management and curriculum study, have also grown up more recently. (See Golby, 1976, and Carr and Kemmis, 1986, for fuller details.) In almost all of these cases, however (apart from curriculum theory), Education is offered insights from other disciplines, the implication being that their theoretical knowledge, coming first, should be used by Education.

From the previous section, however, it will already be apparent that, in addition to seeing theory as something that can be brought to education from elsewhere:

(a) theory is now seen by some as emanating from practice as well as leading to practice
(b) practitioners who reflect upon their practice are theorising, and thus are theorists
(c) anyone who does anything does so on the basis of some theories, though he or she might not have articulated them consciously.

This lays bare the former false distinction between practitioners as those who carried out practice and theorists as those who worked from the Education Theory disciplines to produce theory which was then applied to practice. (One illogicality here is that the so-called theorists were never simply theorists but were also practitioners in their own disciplines – psychology, philosophy, sociology.) The problem was that they were recommending the application of their theories to those engaged in a different practice – teaching.

How, then, might theory now properly be described? A simplistic description might suggest that it is about the generation and refinement of laws, principles, general and universal truths. Or it might be more to do with the interpretation of reasons, patterns, motives, ways of enquiring. For Reid, 1978, p.22, it is any form of modelling (seeing a pattern in) the past, and the present, or of anticipating a pattern in the future. It is also possible to distinguish between theories (principles; interpretations of reasons; ways of enquiring), from over-arching theory (a main system of theory which commonly informs all of one's actions), and meta-theory (theory about theory). But it is not only *what* theory generates that moulds its character. At least as important is *how* this theory-making is approached, and how the theory is expected to be used.

Thus, traditional Education Theory and the extended theoretical perspectives of the additional disciplines generated insights from those disciplines. And the theory-making was done inside those other disciplines by means of their traditional methods of creating knowledge. The relationship of this theory to the practice of schooling was then essentially applicatory, handed down, and disengaged from practice. By contrast, theory out of practice generates insights (largely influenced by currently held theory) as a result of the investigation of practice itself, and compares these insights with other related insights (already known, or newly sought). Here the theory-making is done out of, and as part of, practical problem-solving, and the relationship between theory and practice is essentially interactive.

Reid's seminal work *Thinking About the Curriculum* is useful here. Arguing the case for curriculum research as opposed to educational research, he makes the point that there is an important distintion between 'theory as systematic enquiry, or as the product of systematic enquiry, and theory as idealised practice' (Reid, 1978, p.17). As he argues, until fairly recently, theory as idealised practice has been the predominant version of theory in Education. This traditional view of Education Theory involves theory which is inspired in bystanders and spectators of practice who think up improvements for it. These, as Reid says, 'deduce the consequences of action without actually carrying it out'. This may result in insights and even testable hypotheses, but the situation which this kind of theory assumes frequently does not mirror reality, even in its starting points. It is for this reason that theory has been seen by many practitioners as largely irrelevant or even misleading. It is, as Reid, 1978, p.18 suggests, in a sense in competition with practice.

If this is how theory as idealised practice proceeds, what are the processes of theory as systematic enquiry? This is enquiry into practice. Reid characterises this as 'naturalistic' as opposed to idealistic. It does not set out to say what should be the case in idealised terms (though, of course, it works within a general framework of aspects of eduction that are desirable), but rather it sets out to establish what is in fact the case, in order to 'provide perspectives for understanding how and why things work the way they do', and as the basis for future decision. (See Reid, 1978, p.18.)

This is not as conservative an approach as Carr and Kemmis (1986) suggest. They argue that it does little more than ascertain the details of an individual case of practice. But if the enquirers draw on wider perspectives, other cases and other theory, they can question values, reorder priorities and determine new directions for practice, and can do so within a framework of broadly moral concerns. *This* is the point made about *praxis* above.

Is all practice, are all actions and activities, then, imbued with theory?

Theory out of practice

It is one thing to assert that there is theory lurking in all practice, and another to assert that the practitioner is automatically a theorist. As we have seen above, it is possible for the practitioner to lack all consciousness of that theory which is implicit in his practice (in which case for him it does not seem to exist).

In order that the 'inert theory' which lies beneath the surface of our practice and consciousness can be examined, there are procedures for exhuming it, or in Eisner's metaphor, bringing it to life. These are the procedures of reflection and deliberation which have recently been explicated in some detail by those working in the field of curriculum studies. They are described in detail in Chapter 5.

To do no more than dig theory blindly out of practice, that is, to have no other perspectives to bring up to that practice and its theory, would not actually be possible, since our enquiry methods as well as what we do with our observations of the theory in our practice are themselves dependent on our pre-existing theories about the phenomena in question (Reid, 1978, p.22). Thus, not only is all practice theory-imbued, but all knowledge is theory-impregnated, and all approaches to enquiry have themselves a theoretical basis. What is needed then is only the enquirer and a systematic approach to the enquiry.

Our grounds for taking any action (practical or theoretical) are in order to deal with a situation, resolve it or understand it better. Thus, our problem is not to find whether theory exists in practice or enquiry or knowledge, but to choose (from the theories held and those available) which are the best to seize upon at the time to help us (temporarily) to solve our problem, given our understanding and abilities. To this end, some would argue, what is required is the establishing and the maintaining of a critical (deliberative) tradition within which all proposals for practice can be scrutinised. This is why theoretical and practical perspectives now both can be and need to be drawn closer together than was the case in earlier Educational Theoretical traditions.

The questions, then, remain: is there a natural and unbridgeable gap between practice and theory or not, and is there now a clear-cut view about theory and practice?

The gap, real or unreal?

The simplistic answer to this question is that while there were in the training institutions predominantly Educational Theorists whose approach to practice was of the 'idealised practice' kind described above, and who saw theory as created by theorists in one context and tradition, and applied to practice in another, there seemed to be a fixed void between theory and practice. This void is presently being maintained by two sets of people. It is maintained by those practitioners in the professions whose only experience was of this kind of theory and who continue (understandably) to declare that theory is neither realistic nor relevant to practice. It is also maintained by those theorists who hold that the only way to erode the theory-practice gap is to induce practitioners to accept and apply theories of a kind that are not their own. (It is a grim thought that many government education initiatives come into this category.)

The irony is that many practitioners who maintain their rejection of theory because they see all theory as of the kind that is foisted upon them are often actually involved in the very activities of investigating and reflecting upon their own practice. Thus, without their knowing it, their approach is central to modern views of theory, which are dedicated to bringing theory and practice closer together. Such practitioners have not yet seen that the term 'theory' refers to the whole enterprise of investigating and appraising critically their practice.

What then is the nature of this closer relationship between theory and practice? In a nutshell, it is a bending of both perspectives (the activities of action and of theorising from or in action) which, without blurring their essential and separate natures, can contribute to the solution of practical problems. Ideally, this involves reflection upon practice, followed by deliberation with fellow practitioners (via reading, study, and discussion) about the insights gained.

In these terms then every practitioner can be – and should consciously be – a theorist, and every such individual also needs to belong to a community with whom to deliberate upon the substance of his reflections. If this is so, there are considerable implications for teacher training.

The problematic nature of theory and practice

Of course, there can be no agreement about theory and practice because of the value-based nature of Education itself. How they are viewed largely depends upon what perceptions and knowledge and values are brought up to them by the viewer. There is not even agreement about whether or not they are problematic, since for some, knowledge (including knowledge about theory and practice) is absolute and given, while for others it is temporary and multifaceted. Such a lack of agreement about these matters leads to a number of significant dilemmas, including the following.

Some present dilemmas about professional practice

The following three questions demonstrate some common dilemmas which have to be faced by those seeking to investigate and improve practice.

What kind of activity is teaching?

A simplistic view of the nature of teaching is that it is either made up of simple skills or is an activity which is complex, cannot be defined, and which can therefore only be learnt by doing.

A more useful approach is to consider the nature of the activities involved in teaching. Where teaching is seen as an activity which is predominantly skill-based, rational and logical, and reducible to specific categories which can therefore be learnt by simply practising a number of skills or mastering the categories, it is seen to be of a rational-logical or scientific nature. That is, its activities are essentially technical. Such a view of teaching is implicit in a number of government documents about the curriculum and about teacher appraisal. Practice is regarded as a matter of putting into operation a number of routines and applying theory.

If, however, teaching is seen as something not so easily reduced, but which yields to broader interpretation in which human rather than simply logical factors need to be considered, and in which capacities, knowledge, personality, understanding, habits and competences play a creative part, then it is seen as artistic in nature. Much of teaching actually involves both sorts of activity, and creativity is an essential element in many scientific discoveries.

But this does not negate some crucial differences.

Many of the central decisions and judgements made during professional training about the trainer's methods, the course content and means of assessment (and, also, in the case of teacher training, made in the *student's* choice of methods, content and means of assessment) rest upon these crucial distinctions. From this issue flow many controversies and misunderstandings which need to be aired rather than suppressed by those seeking to work together towards professional development.

For this reason the following model has been developed as an aid to identifying for each view both the different vocabulary used and the significant concepts and their underlying assumptions and values. This is no more than an attempt to indicate the kind of issues which need to be considered. For a further discussion of this matter, see Eisner (1983), pp.4–13; Langford (1985); Stenhouse (1980).

Whether teaching is seen as a scientific (a technical-rational) activity or as one of the arts (involving creative activities) can be detected in the following statements. These are presented in crude dichotomies only in order to make the point clearly.

- Science seeks rules, principles, laws; art starts where rules fade, and prefers guides.
- Science uses diagnosis, analysis, prescription; art offers interpretation, exploration.
- Science uses schedules, follows detailed pre-planning; art prefers rules of thumb, spontaneity.
- Science offers the learner mainly skills and information; art sees learning as better facilitated by means of structures and patterns.
- Science rests on routines; art moves quickly to improvisations.
- Science demands closed, efficient systems; art provides room for imagination. (NB This is not to say that creativity and imagination are absent from science.)
- Science can reduce all learners to the same by stressing the similar aspects of routines; art will increase the differences by stressing individual interpretation and creativity.
- Science uses task analysis to help determine what the learner will need; art suggests imagining yourself as the learner.
- Science sees people as puppets and receivers; the arts see people as negotiators of new meanings, understandings.
- Science talks about motivation, feedback, 'failed input'; art talks about how humans react, respond.
- Science sees learning as stemming from efficient teaching; the arts see learning as not actually logically related to teaching at all.
- Science sees knowledge as static, attainable, absolute; art sees knowledge as temporary, dynamic, only able to be grasped at.
- Science bases knowledge about teaching and learning on the scientific disciplines of psychology and sociology and linguistics; the arts base

such knowledge on understandings gleaned from art, literature, history, philosophy.
- Science assumes (Education) Theory *is* scientific theory; the arts allow such theory to be personal – created via a mixture and range of humanities including literature, art, history, autobiography and certain approaches of sociology.
- Science refers to aims, behavioural objectives; art prefers intentions, goals.
- Science talks about feedback loops; the arts listen to expressive nuance.
- Science talks about reinforcement, manipulation; the arts prefer the ability to read other human beings and their actions and to work *with* rather than on them.
- Science offers prescriptions; the arts offer guides.
- Science sees education as fostered by scientific (industrial) management; the arts see it as fostered by being sensitive to and valuing people, and developing self-management and self-appraisal.
- Science brings to educational thinking an atomising and analytical approach; the arts function by means of critical appreciation.

(see Fish, 1988, pp.27–28)

It will quickly be clear that these differing approaches, values and beliefs will result in very different kinds of training. And, of course, it should be clear that on occasions this is not a straight dichotomy, but a question of making a series of choices at each decision-making point in design, evaluation, investigation or appraisal.

However, considering teaching is not enough. The emphasis today is upon enabling learning. Thus, although the activity of teaching is *not* logically related to that of learning, it nevertheless needs to be considered in relation to it. The following question, therefore, needs to be asked.

What kind of activity is learning?

In spite of all the knowledge which traditional Educational Theory has generated on this topic, there is still much that we are unsure of here. The popular view is that if successful teaching has taken place then learning will automatically follow for all. Many prefer not to question whether it is possible for teaching to happen without any learning (which, logically, it is). And in our egalitarian society many have been dissuaded from questioning whether everyone is actually capable of the same learning.

If that is the popular view, then the views expressed by those who have studied learning in detail are much less cohesive. Just as for the activity of teaching, there are some who will maintain that learning will yield to certain laws and routines which will (for example) enhance motivation, improve memory, and increase learning. (See Stones, 1984.) For others, learning is a complex activity which is better addressed from a wider and more humanistic position where what is not known can be as comfortably acknowledged as what is known. (See Barrow, 1984, Chapter 7.)

What theory do teachers need to know?

Those in favour of formal Education Theory will argue that as part of their basic education teachers (and therefore students) need to be acquainted with the hard facts about education across the Education disciplines; that these will yield insights into the nature of teaching and learning; that it is important to be aware of the major issues and to think about them in isolation from the bustle of the classroom and school; and that it is important to seek to keep uncertainty at bay.

Those in favour of a more practical-based theory will argue that the hard facts of theory are not always either reliable or generally applicable to practice; that theory does not confront the substantive issues of how to provide the kinds of information which can lead to better decision-making in the classroom about what should be taught and learnt (Reid, 1978, p.26); that the research is often contradictory, and that what is called theory is often little more than 'a loose network of fashion, fantasy, political motives, general ideas and various research findings' (Wilson, 1975, p.117). This is perhaps because it is not clear where the central issues of educational research lie. This, in turn, may be because as Reid argues, Educational Theory takes its coherence not from a central issue, but from attempts to invest Education with disciplinary status via the advancement of various research techniques. (See Reid, 1978, p.26.)

Those like Reid, therefore, argue powerfully that what is needed by teachers are practical principles which are not provided by foundation Theory; and that Theory needs to be subsumed in a problem-orientated, theoretical framework which is relevant and easily related to practice. In these respects, Education Theory has nothing to tell teachers of 'average insight, competence and understanding' which is not 'demonstrably correct, practically useful and that they don't know already'. (See Wilson, 1975, p.118.)

Thus, some will argue, what teachers need is knowledge of the principles of enquiry, reflection, and deliberation, and the capacity and understanding to be conceptually alert to the problems of practice. This is because effective practice turns upon effective decision-making, which is a kind of problem-solving. (See Reid, 1978, p.41.) What Reid is arguing for, then, as the knowledge base for a teacher, is curriculum theory and research, which concerns itself with how to solve practical curriculum problems, and with processes of curriculum enquiry. This involves new styles of theorising, and new ways of generating data.

There are also some who would argue that while the most useful kind of theory for practitioners is that which is centred upon practice, there is good reason also to enable students to grasp how the disciplines which make up the so-called foundation disciplines of Education actually work. But where this is a plea for an epistemological approach to determine the structures and procedures of Educational Theory itself, this can be achieved through learning about enquiry methods.

The above ideas now enable us to define five views of theory and practice.

Five views of theory and practice

The following model, which owes much to Schön, 1987b, pp.26–40, and something to Tom, 1987, shows how five differing views of theory and practice stem from:

- differing views of knowledge itself
- differing views about the knowledge base necessary to practical competence
- differing ideas about the relationship of that knowledge to practical competence
- differing views about how to develop practical competence
- differing attitudes to the reality of professional practice.

In practice, these views result in differing sorts of professional activity.

All of these views can be found in most institutions. The five might best be characterised as: *intuitive; common-sense; applicatory; creative*; and *reconstructionist* views.

The intuitive view

The intuitive view essentially dismisses knowledge. It holds the following to be the case:

- that procedural knowledge (knowledge how) is unrelated to learning to teach
- that propositional knowledge (knowledge that) is insignificant and therefore irrelevant to professional practice
- that uninvestigated experience is the only necessary basis for teaching
- that teaching is not really based upon any theory
- that the ability to teach is innate and cannot really be taught
- that incidentally, therefore, practice is unrefinable except by repetition or luck
- that professional reality can be subdued, tamed, and will automatically submit to the innate talent that the teacher brings to it.

The professional activity often associated with this view is the unquestioning repetition of what works and the unpredictable 'bran-tub' approach to new situations (where a response to the situation is pulled blindly out of the unknown and might, or might not, prove to be a lucky dip).

The common-sense view

The common-sense view holds the following to be the case:

- that the most useful practical knowledge resides in tradition
- that the knowledge necessary to practical competence is tips for teachers which come from the craft experience of those already involved

- that the simple knowledge of these tips will provide a sound basis for successful practice, providing enough time is devoted to putting them into practice
- that plenty of practice is naturally good
- that real practice is always the same underneath and will yield to the known formula.

This results in a style of teaching which does not change with the times and which has little opportunity of adapting to changes in schools and society.

The applicatory view

The applicatory view holds the following to be the case:

- that knowledge is objective and absolute
- that the proper basis for teaching (or any activity) is pre-learnt, propositional knowledge (theory)
- that such theory should be learnt and then applied to practice
- that improving practice is a matter of improving theory
- that the reality of professional practice is that it will yield to theory once the right theory is used.

The activities most often associated with this view include adopting the latest bandwagon, a seeking of technical mastery over routines, and a slavery to propositional knowledge and those who peddle it.

The creative view

The creative view holds the following to be the case:

- that knowledge is relative rather than absolute, that it is temporary and refinable, and that its value base should be acknowledged
- that it is not pre-made by theorists but is constructable by the practitioner
- that such an ongoing process of construction and an awareness of this process and its value base is a vital element in both doing and refining practice
- that professional reality, being unpredictable and unique, can best be met by a creative approach.

The activities most associated with this approach include the active investigation of his own practice by the practitioner; improvisation and experimentation; and what Schön refers to as holding a conversation with the situation (Schön, 1987b, p.31).

The reconstructionist view

The reconstructionist view holds the following to be the case:

- that the approach of those holding the creative view, though right in some respects, is essentially conservative in intent, and so does not go far enough

- that the creative view of the nature of knowledge and its relationship to practical competence is acceptable
- but that the development of practical competence should include developing perspectives on the value base of the practitioner, professional practice and society, and on how to reform professional practice and its world according to Marxist ideology.

Its attitude to professional reality, therefore, is that it should, as part of society, be reconstructed to fit Marxist ideals. The activities associated with this view, although they usefully call attention to the possible parochial aspects of the creative view, also essentially involve a particular manipulation of people and ideas which is unacceptable to some.

Some comments

Clearly, the first three of these are essentially of an earlier age. The fourth, the creative approach, has been charged with holding a myopic view of education in that its concern is with the immediate realities of practice – usually in the classroom. However, as we shall see below, it is possible to couple this approach with one which leads to a wider view. The reconstructionist view, as implied above, though usefully calling our attention to the shortcomings of the creative view, has a particular indoctrinating intention.

The existence, in practice, of some of these views has recently been shown in a small survey conducted across two London boroughs of teachers in primary and secondary schools who were particularly experienced in working with students on teacher-training courses.

In response to a question about the role of theory in learning to teach, asked during an individual hour-long interview, only 4 out of 50 teachers queried the exact meaning of the word theory, and all of these assumed it to mean Education Theory as they had met it in their own training. The place of theory was seen as central to practice by only 15 of the 50. It was seen as to be applied to practice by a further 13, and was seen as irrelevant to practice by 22 (ie, nearly half). Not one respondent suggested that the kind of 'lesson analysis' or 'lesson "crit"' (that they had been talking about in response to an earlier question) actually involved drawing on a range of theoretical perspectives or could enable the drawing out of a range of theory *from* the student's practice. Neither did anyone suggest that any theory might influence lesson debriefing, offer perspectives during the debriefing, or be examined in the debriefing.

Clearly, these teachers did not have at their disposal any meta-theory about debriefing, reflection, deliberation or the relationship of theory and practice. Neither did they see the activities of debriefing as relating to or as worthy of being called 'Theory'. For them, Theory was exclusively the province of the training institutions and emerged from the foundation disciplines of Education.

Further, it should be said, there is little evidence that college tutors are themselves necessarily able to be greatly articulate about the details of how theory can contribute to the training of teachers. Work by the College of St

Paul and St Mary on tutors' supervision seems to support this view. (See Terrell, Mathis, Winstanley and Wright, 1986.)

The implications for professional training of these five views of theory and practice will be obvious. Indeed, these models may be of use to course design teams and to individual triads in establishing and refining their approach to partnership. Further, the implications of each model will affect work at two levels. The views about theory and practice will determine views about teaching and learning themselves and about learning to teach and the processes of professional training. Thus, those who subscribe to the applicatory view will expect to apply theory to teaching and to training, while those who hold the creative view will expect to construct their understanding of both teaching and training as they proceed.

The following is an appraisal, made from a creative or constructionist viewpoint, of the new perspectives currently emerging on professional training.

5. Reconceptualising Professional Training: A New Basis for Learning to Teach

Summary

- Some ideas about theory and practice
  - the role of theory in professional training
  - new ways of conceptualising practice
  - improvisation as an example
- Some approaches to learning through practice
  - investigation
  - the scientific tradition of investigation
  - the humanistic tradition
  - five approaches to reflection
  - an example of the results of reflection
  - debriefing as a means of fostering reflection
  - deliberation (or practical reasoning)

Introduction

For those adhering to the traditional applicatory view of theory and practice, approaches to professional training are relatively clear-cut. But what perspectives exist for those who would subscribe to a creative or constructionist view? What knowledge and what procedures would be helpful to the enterprise of training? What basis might there be for fostering the student's learning through practice? In this case, the propositional knowledge from Education Theory becomes the background to more central procedural knowledge about solving practical problems. And the application of Education Theory is replaced by techniques for investigating practice, reflecting upon it and deliberating about it. The following is an attempt to offer some useful perspectives upon these.

Some ideas about theory and practice

The role of theory in professional training

It is *not* being suggested in any of the above that theory is no longer necessary for and is no longer related to practice. What is implied, however, is that a different kind of theory is now useful in training for professional practice, and that it plays a different role. As Reid (1978), pp.22–24 suggests, in trying to understand a practical situation we are influenced by our pre-formed theories and previous practices. In the solving of our practical problems we evolve theory from our insight into the problem. We do this by bringing our previous and present practical experience and our previous and relevant new theoretical understanding together until they are mutually accommodated in a solution to the problem which in some sense 'fits' both previous and newly-sought theory and previous and present practice. Since the only solution to practical problems is demonstrated by action, we carry out an appropriate action (sometimes in the middle of our theorising), and thus provide ourselves with further data to process in the same way again by means of reflection and deliberation. We also draw upon knowledge of how to look up or search for related knowledge from other fields, and how those fields work in terms of their assumptions, concerns, values, logic, procedures, and evidence.

From this it will rapidly become clear that the methods of enquiry into practice, and processes of reflection and deliberation about practice, together with some basic knowledge of Educational Theory and particularly epistemology, have become the likely theoretical basis of this approach to professional training. Thus, all those involved in training need to be fully cognisant of them.

New ways of conceptualising practice

The work of Schön (1987b) and Woods (1987) has provided us with some useful ways of thinking about practice. Woods argues for 'a new conception of knowledge' which is:

> not simply an extant body of facts and theories but a living, experiential, processual, flexible, creative compilation of insights, memories, information, associations, articulations that go into resourcing on-the-spot teacher decision-making and action. (Woods, 1987, p.122)

He argues that this will include many ambiguities, inconsistencies, and contradictions as well as empirical and observable facts and emotions. The vehicle which he argues can be used to facilitate this is the narrating of teachers' life histories. This point is taken up in more detail below.

But it is Schön (1987b) who has provided us with more specific ideas. He talks about professional artistry, which he argues refers to the 'kinds of competence practitioners sometimes display in unique, uncertain and conflicted situations of practice'. This is a high-powered version of what is known as 'skillful performance' (Schön, 1987b, p.22). He offers his terms 'knowing-in-action' and 'reflection-in-action' as useful ways of referring to the sorts of knowledge revealed in intelligent action, Schön, 1987b, p.25). Particularly useful also is his consideration of improvisation, which, he argues persuasively, is at the heart of the response of the professional to unpredictable practical problems.

Improvisation as an example

Schön reminds us that improvisation in jazz is a matter of the musicians listening to themselves and each other and feeling their way into the performance where they vary, combine, and recombine a certain set of figures within a schema or framework (metre, melody, harmonic development) which gives coherence to the whole. This process, Schön says:

> resembles the familiar patterns of everyday conversation. In a good conversation – in some respects predictable and in others not – participants pick up and develop themes of talk, each spinning out variations on her repertoire of things to say. Conversation is collective verbal improvisation. At times it falls into conventional routines – the ancedote with the side comments and reactions, for example, or the debate – which develop according to a pace and rhythm of interaction that the participants seem, without conscious deliberation, to work out in common within the framework of an evolving division of labor. At other times, there may be surprises, unexpected turns of phrase or directions of development to which participants invent on-the-spot responses. (Schön, 1987b, p.30)

The notion of variations within a framework raises interesting questions for professional practice about what framework is required, how it is established, and how the variations arise.

Some approaches to learning through practice

Investigation

Investigation, except where it is an end in itself, is a key means of learning about practice. Further, not all of its approaches are useful to the individual practitioner working to learn through practice.

For some, educational investigation is essentially about a search for scientific laws and generalisations based upon objective evidence and quantitative analysis. These investigators work in the scientific tradition, and expect their findings to be applied to practice. For others, the process of enquiry must involve a wider investigation. It starts from practice and draws upon a range of perspectives to gain access to a more complete, complex, and inevitably subjective picture. Here the research tradition is the humanistic one and the resulting data is qualitative.

The scientific tradition of investigation

As Carr and Kemmis (1986), p.56 point out, the emergence of Education Theory from the nineteenth century into the twentieth brought with it the idea that Education would best progress by allegiance to the scientific approach, although early on it also retained the idea, from earlier philosophical thinking, that the value of theory lay 'in its capacity to enlighten practice'. Broadly speaking, however, the scientific (positivist or rationalist) approach seemed to determine the organisation and procedures of Educational Theory and research.

From their early stages, the psychology and the sociology of Education saw themselves as working centrally in the tradition of behaviourism. Their aim was to find laws and principles which should be applied in the schools. To do so they worked within scientific traditions by means of establishing hypotheses as the basis for research activity, and then seeking empirical evidence from people's behaviour. This evidence they assumed was itself simple and was susceptible to one simple interpretation which in turn could be converted to figures that were statistically valid.

These approaches found it helpful, therefore, to conceive of various educational activities (for example, teaching and learning) as reducible to laws and principles and as scientific in nature. That is, they took a reductionist view of human life, assuming that it could be easily reduced to categories. The advantages of this, as they saw it, were that the subject of investigation was reducible to clear evidence and that this evidence (and their findings from it) was objective and therefore significant; and also generalisable and therefore applicable to practice. Further, it could take place on a large scale, which was popular with administrators and impressive in the eyes of the public. However, problems soon arose when different research teams investigating similar aspects came up with different conclusions.

The claim made for this approach to investigation was that it sought and produced hard facts. The behaviourist basis of their thinking assumed that what could be observed was both objective and indisputable evidence of indisputable facts. In short, learning was seen as an activity whose existence was able to be affirmed by observable behaviour. This view also included the belief that the activities observed and reduced to simple evidence represented equally simple and incontrovertible truths. The interpretation of these facts into truths was also considered accurate and objective. Knowledge, too, was seen as fixed and eternal, rather than tentative and temporary. Thus, in the end, this scientific approach began to prove itself narrower than the scientific origins from which it had come.

It nevertheless still holds sway among many in the main fields of psychology and sociology of education and linguistics, and has great attraction for theorists and administrators alike in that it offers clear-cut thinking and provides for straightforward decision-making – some would say at the expense of recognising the human dimensions of human activity.

Particularly, this approach can be seen in what are sometimes known as evaluation instruments and techniques. Here, it exists in a range of schedules, interaction grids, statistically interpreted questionnaires, and a range of instruments designed to measure educational phenomena and produce quantitative data. It is also beginning to provide the instruments for appraisal and self-appraisal.

The humanistic tradition

In contrast to the above tradition is the humanistic, or interpretive or qualitative, approach to theory-making, research, investigation and evaluation.

This approach, which has in the 1980s sought to compete with, if not replace, the scientific tradition, has emerged from the phenomenological approach of the sociology of education. Basically it attempts to take account of the very subjectivity which the behaviourists, in their 'objective' interpretations, ignore or pretend does not exist. At its most conservative it does this by trying to bring into central focus all the very human and complex features that the scientific approach either ignored or tried to neutralise.

It is found at its most extreme in ethnomethodological approaches. (Ethnology means the investigation of *varieties* of the human race.) This approach takes as its starting point the questioning of even the most basic assumptions about the sharing of meanings in the social interaction being investigated. This can sometimes reveal frightening gaps in understanding between a group of human beings who have been wrongly assuming that the group has one shared perception of meanings and events, when in fact it has as many as the number in the group. In this way it takes as problematic many of the issues and interpretations and definitions that the scientific approach has assumed as agreed and unimportant and ignorable. In its revelations about the problematic nature of education, it has laid the ground for wider investigation.

Here, then, is a very different view of investigation which opens the way to a lone investigator studying one case. Further, it is encouraged to be idiosyncratic, highly conscious of its subjective judgements, and it is not necessarily able to lead to laws and general principles which can be applied to other practitioners, although it can have influence on their work.

If these are some of the approaches to investigating practice, what do we know about the processes of reflecting upon these procedures and upon the data they produce?

Five approaches to reflection

Dewey, of course, like Aristotle before him, recognised the importance of reflection. In *How We Think* (1933), Dewey wrote of the importance of conscious reflective activity. There are now several sets of approach to reflection, though they all owe allegiance to Dewey's work. Five of the most interesting, in chronological order are:

- ideas about reflection across a number of professional fields as presented by Boud, Keogh and Walker in 1985
- the teacher-as-researcher model as explored by Carr and Kemmis (1986)
- an approach via autobiography as written about by Pinar (1986), but also discussed by Eisner (1985), and Woods (1987)
- reflection-in-action, as explored by Schön (1987b)

– teacher as self-appraiser as described by Pollard and Tann (1987).

The view about reflection enunciated by Boud, Keogh and Walker, though somewhat general, is very useful. In their introduction to *Reflection: Turning Experience into Learning* they helpfully elucidate three stages of reflection: the preparation, the engagement in activity, and the processing of what has been experienced (Boud, Keogh and Walker, 1985, p.9).

The preparatory stage, they argue, should contain four parts:

- an outline by the supervisor of the aims of the activity and the broad structure of what is to take place
- the opportunity for students to clarify and even modify what has been suggested
- the pre-practising of the skills required of them in a sheltered college setting
- an introduction to the resources available to assist them during the period of practical experience.

Throughout these, reflection occurs as the students explore what is required of them, the demands of the field, and the resources available, including what they themselves bring.

During the field experience students often resort to coping strategies and may never, in the short term, come to grips with the relationship between theory and practice. This may come only later after considerable debriefing. Here, interestingly, the authors seem less than fully aware of the enormous potential of the students' recording of field events as they happen. However, they do say that all the students will have made:

> various kinds of note and records of their experience. For some this may ... (be) systematic laboratory notebooks, for others it might have consisted of jottings of events, remarks, questions and thoughts. The input of information is considerable, and students have to draw back from being totally immersed in the experience in order to digest what is happening. This may involve withdrawing for a time from the task ... or trying to make sense of what is happening through keeping a personal diary to record issues, feelings and value conflicts. (Boud, Keogh and Walker, 1985, p.10)

What they do not perhaps stress enough, however, is the value of the written responses themselves as a learning process, and what can be gained from revisiting them later.

During the debriefing phase, they argue, students should report on their experiences by referring to their notes and their memories and trying to reconstruct an account of the salient features of the experience. 'In this process', say Boud, Keogh and Walker, 'the students will realize many things left undone, questions unasked and records incomplete. All this is part of the learning process.' (Boud, Keogh and Walker, 1985, p.10.) They maintain that the goal of reconstructing the experience is most important, because:

> in order to pursue this goal ... learners need to describe their experience, to work

through the attitude and emotions which might colour their understanding, and to order and make sense of the new ideas and information which they have retained. (Boud, Keogh and Walker, 1985, p.11)

In addition to these points, they make three other very significant ones:

1. No one can learn for anyone else, and only learners can reflect on their own experiences.
2. Reflection of this kind is pursued with intent, and is not idle meanderings.
3. Reflective processes are complex and involve both feelings and cognition.

More detailed ideas are to be found in the work of Carr and Kemmis. Here, working more overtly towards a reconstructionist approach, Carr and Kemmis raise issues about the values brought by student and supervisor. Their key stages include the following:

1. before teaching the student explains, explicitly on paper, her beliefs, priorities, the intentions of her teaching and of her planning for teaching
2. after the lesson the student explains the actual practice, *and then justifies it* (initially to a teacher or tutor and ultimately to herself)
3. the student then examines critically the beliefs and assumptions inherent in her actual practice *and* her explication of it
4. the student then compares these beliefs, values, assumptions with:
   - her previously stated beliefs
   - the collegiate version of the traditions of the profession in this respect
   - the relevant knowledge generated by Educational Theory and any other related fields.

The student does this with a view to making a further critical appraisal of the *adequacy* of her concepts, beliefs, assumptions, and values in illuminating and refining her practice.

In all of this there is the opportunity to exhume and face a number of important issues which are normally suppressed. These might include:

- the frustrations, limitations, and constraints and coercions which bear upon the action
- the routines, habits, customs, traditions, ideologies, dogmas, prejudices, certainties, precedents which are brought to the action and the decision about-action-in-action
- the influences upon the investigation of the action, and its associated interpretations, judgements, and decisions.

This, then, is a model which enables the practitioner to delve deeply into his educational thinking and understanding as well as to take account of some external influences and constraints.

This approach is not dissimilar to the recent work of Pollard and Tann

(1987), which tends to see reflection as a tool of self-appraisal. For them reflective teaching:

- implies an active concern with aims and consequences as well as means and technical efficiency
- combines enquiry and implementation skills with attitudes of open-mindedness, responsibility and wholeheartedness
- is applied in a cyclical or spiralling process in which teachers continually monitor, evaluate, and revise their own practice
- is based upon teacher judgement, informed partly by self-reflection and partly by insights from the educational disciplines.
(Pollard and Tann, 1987, p.3)

A quite different approach to reflection is found in the idea of autobiography as reflection. This idea is usefully discussed by Pinar (1986), and Woods (1987). Woods makes the case for what he calls life histories by saying that they are an eminently suitable method in the compilation of teacher knowledge, based as they are within the subjective reality of the individual (Woods, 1987, p.124). They are, he says, personal documents yet at the same time, by attending to the variety of contexts (historical, political, social), they also offer a fully contextualised view (p.131). He argues too that they have a reinterpretational value in that for the individual, they 'bring meaning to extant bodies of knowledge and disciplines that otherwise would be seen by teachers as not only irrelevant but alien' (p.125).

These ideas are to be found in the work of Pinar, who, again, works in the reconstructionist tradition. The following three passages give the flavour of his work:

> Autobiographical method offers opportunities to return to our own situations, our 'rough edges', to reconstruct our intellectual agendas. The focus in such work is the felt problematic; its method is intuitive. One falls back on oneself – rather than upon the words of others – and must articulate what is yet unspoken, act as midwife to the unborn . . . (Pinar, 1986, p.33)

> What we aspire to . . . is not adherence to conventions of a literary form. Nor do we think of audience, of portraying our life to others. We write autobiography for ourselves, in order to cultivate our capacity to see through the outer forms, the habitual explanations of things, the stories we tell in order to keep others at a distance. It is against the taken-for-granted, against routine and ritual we work . . .(Pinar, 1986, p.34)

> Autobigraphical method . . . reconstructs the past, as it lays bare the relation between self and work (and) self and others which has prevailed in the past. (Pinar, 1986, p.35)

By contrast to this autobiographical approach, the work of Schön concentrates upon looking more closely at the detailed processes of what he calls 're-flection-in-action'. This occurs when we stop and reflect during action. When we discover a problem during action we invent procedures to solve the problem. This is what we sometimes call trial and error. But, as Schön points out:

> the trials are not randomly related to one another; reflection on each trial and its results sets the stage for the next trial. Such a pattern of enquiry is better described as a sequence of 'moments' in a process of reflection-in-action. (Schön, 1987b, p.27)

Schön goes on to argue that reflection-in-action is a critical questioning of our knowledge in action and its assumptions. It includes thinking critically about the very thinking which took us into the problem in the first place, and can lead to the restructuring of ideas, attitudes, understandings. He points out that what distinguishes reflection-in-action from other sorts of reflection is its 'immediate significance for action' (Schön, 1987b, p.29). The implication is that this is a continuous process of on-the-spot experiment and thought. A skilled performer, Schön argues, can integrate reflection-in-action into a smooth performance. He also points out that the ability to be skilful in this way is not necessarily related to being able to talk about it.

All of the approaches described above have something to offer the practitioner and the trainee who is trying to understand and improve practice. And they all share the basic notion that attempting to describe and interpret what is happening or has happened can be a very good way of understanding it better. The example below illustrates this.

An example of the results of reflection

The following is taken direct from the school experience notebook of DJ, a postgraduate student who qualified as a teacher in July 1986. It demonstrates much of what Pinar was expressing above, and is included as a demonstration of the power of personal writing to aid a student's reflection upon practical experience. This student was writing about one part of a day visit to a community school in outer London. He had made eight out of ten such weekly visits at this point. The account comes from the diary which he was required to keep as part of this course, and so this account was written at least partly with a tutor in mind.

Feb 6th 1986

Special Needs

We had been asked to prepare worksheets for special needs work by BD, the head of the school's Learning Development Department. We worked with children withdrawn for extra language help . . . Our worksheets were based on Ladybird books we had borrowed. I wanted 'The Three Billy Goats Gruff', but Robert pinched it so I had to make do with 'Rumpelstiltskin'. This was little short of tragic. The attempt to simplify the story has in this case made it largely meaningless. Rumpelstiltskin, in this version, stamps his foot when his name is guessed, but only manages to get his leg stuck between floorboards. He eventually frees it and stomps off in a huff. The devil trying to ensnare a human soul is thus reduced to a pint-sized philanthropist given to bouts of incomprehensible behaviour. The text itself is very undemanding – short basic sentence structure and simple vocabulary (king, gold, straw) but with the one remarkable exception – *mannikin*!! This damn word crops up again and again.

It made the production of worksheets extremely difficult. In the end I produced a ten-sentence prose sequence and a cloze-procedure (with a list of words to be filled in) – beautiful multicoloured affairs in nice clear writing. Lakbinder read me the story, stumbling over only 'mannikin' (I could have choked), and then did the worksheets. They were neither too hard nor too easy and filled the time nicely. She coped particularly well with the sequence work... She had more trouble with the easy cloze-procedure, getting in a muddle half-way through, suggesting wholly inappropriate words and looking blank. We got there in the end.... Finally, curious to discover what she made of the story, I asked her why she thought Rumpelstiltskin wanted the baby. After a moment's deliberation she said: 'Perhaps because he was lonely'. Strong shades of *Silas Marner* here – editors of Ladybird books beware. I got on very well with Lakbinder. EF (the college tutor) came over and said it looked as if it was going very well, and when she had gone my pupil whispered: 'It's all very well for her, she doesn't have to do these sheets!'

All in all it was a very interesting and rewarding experience. Lakbinder's problem, in my view, is a lack of confidence in her own judgement. Her first instinct is most often correct but then she back-pedals, constantly looking at me to confirm her choice BEFORE she has made it. This made for an interesting tactical game. Obviously having decided that what she needs is confidence in her own ability, what I want for her is to commit herself early, when I know she has got it right, so that I can encourage, support, applaud. But she wants all that before she takes the risk. If I allow myself to be drawn in (not into doing the work – she is clearly doing that – but into removing the risk), I will defeat the object. Smiling at her when she smiles interrogatively at me, does not provide the support she thinks she needs. The game than enters a new phase – she drops her immediate (correct) answer and selects another (at random, so it seems to me – always well off the mark). The wrong answer is then put forward with a shrug, a grimace or some such dismissive gesture – she seems at pains to communicate to me her awareness that the answer is wrong, while in the very act of declaring that it is right. If I still hold out eg: 'Is that the right one?', she tries to draw me by making to print the wrong answer indelibly on my beautiful worksheet. Crafty move. I find myself wishing I had brought duplicates. I decide to sacrifice the worksheet and stick to my guns. Now she is trapped. She prints the answer and sits staring at it.

She knows it is wrong. She knows that I know that she knows that it is wrong. I know this because she isn't looking at me – doesn't need to. At this point I intervene slightly: 'What's up?', and succeed in prompting her to commit herself a second time. She challenges me with the assertion: 'It's wrong.' I am now in a position to support her. – 'Yes.' (At this she makes a pantomimic gesture of disappointment – charming, but insincere – she is staying in character. Perhaps she is worried that I will think it naughty of her to put down an answer she knows to be wrong. Had I said the answer was right, I am sure I would have seen real bewilderment.)

So there has been a breakthrough. We are both happy – she because her feet are for the moment on the ground (I have declared the answer wrong) and I because she said it before I did. At the level we are working on, the subject matter (the worksheet) is fast receding in importance. Things are looking up. I find this whole thing a strange and painful state of affairs – that she should sacrifice the chance of being right for the security and comfort of knowing she is wrong. It is particularly irksome, since she had the correct answer in the first place. What I want her to do is pluck up courage and announce the right answer. (Now she feels safe being wrong it may give her the confidence to go one better.)

She doesn't – nor does she select another wrong answer and repeat the process: that's something. She looks as though she could be plucking up courage but she could equally well be thinking about her dinner. Perhaps she HAS really lost sight of the right answer – and who could blame her after a fifteen-minute mind-game with a devious old cynic like me? This possibility looms large – and what with 'Time's winged chariot', I now find myself seeking reassurance.

'I think you know the right answer.'

She grins. I am reassured. She crosses out the old one. The suspense is killing me. She grins again. I grin. She writes down the correct answer. (Thank God for that.) Much encouragement and reward ensues. I put it to her (very pleasantly) that she knew the right answer all along. She agrees, smilingly. I suggest, smilingly, and without a trace of sarcasm in my voice, that it might be a good plan, if we are going to finish in time, if in future we take a short cut and start with the right answers. Put like that, she agrees.

But the act of committing herself clearly makes her feel uncomfortable. By the end of the session it is easier for her – after all she keeps getting the right answers. But it is clearly hard work. Her remark about EF: 'It's all right for her . . . ' was delivered with some feeling and she was probably exhausted for the rest of the day. I was. (DJ)

This work certainly provides a rich description of the occasion at the level of the pupil's and teacher's thought process, or supposed processes. It is original, insightful and carries in its tone the enjoyment of discovering one's own theoretical perspectives instead of having to apply another's. As such, it provided extensive material for further discussion at a debriefing session where various questions of justification arose as well as of teaching and learning strategies. This is an example of what Rowland means when he says: 'By describing rather than by nakedly theorising, we gain an insight into a child's mind.' (Rowland, 1984, p.147.) Further detailed examples of this kind of reflection, and the issues that they raise, are provided in a number of chapters below.

One means of enabling students to reflect in this way is by debriefing them after practical experience.

Debriefing as a means of fostering reflection

Debriefing is taken to mean offering the learner the means of reflecting aloud on the experience and sharing those reflections with others who have been involved. Debriefing clearly needs to be closely related in time to the action itself, and may serve to collect most of the material on which later reflections depend. It should not be overlooked, therefore, that this debriefing in itself establishes the direction and the basic interpretation of the action, though it is possible for individuals later to dissent personally from this initial interpretation. It can be of the greatest help when the person doing the debriefing has witnessed the actual experience, and has been a participant in it. The debriefer may also bring his own observations to bear upon the discussion.

The following ten principles are offered as guides or rules of thumb. The debriefer will need as he works to reflect upon his practice with a view to formulating, as he goes, a working theory for the situation in which he finds himself. Thus, he will rapidly, and properly, proceed beyond the framework offered here.

1. Experiencing something does not mean seeing in it all its implications. Indeed, there will be a wider range of implications than the debriefer will probably have seen. But what is obvious to the person who set up the experience will not be obvious to those who have been struggling to make sense of it. Debriefing, therefore, is a necessary process for experiential learning.
2. The learner should describe in careful detail all the processes she has just been through. The more willing the learner is to think aloud about these processes, the more she will see in them.
3. The thinking which was part of the setting up of the learning activity is as important to consider as is the learner's own decision-making in action. Encourage the learner to distinguish between what she was given in the way of ideas, strategies, rules, by the way the experience was set up, and those which she subsequently reached or found for herself. Lead the learner to raise questions about the validity and nature of what she invented, and what she was given. Encourage the learner to consider the procedures involved in her inventions.
4. It is useful to focus particularly upon the way the learner responded in, or to, the unexpected aspects of the experience. Encourage her to exhume the processes of her own thinking and to look at how she responded and what she relied upon at these points.
5. It is useful to encourage discussion of the learner's affective responses. How did she feel before the experience as she looked towards it? How did she feel during it about the processes, about herself, her co-learners, and the teacher? How does she see herself as a learner in learning through practice?
6. It is useful to focus the learner's attention upon what she has done, and what theoretical assumptions this reveals. What personal theories has she proceeded upon? Where did they come from? How useful were they? How might she modify them in the light of experience and further thought? Encourage the *recognition* of those theories of action present within the learner's activity and the development of further tentative theories for later action.
7. It is useful to draw out the relationship between theory and practice apparent in the situation experienced. What theory was offered? What has the learner invented or brought along from her own reserves? When, during the experience, did she find herself thinking? What does

this tell us all about the relationship of thinking and doing? (A similar process might be applied, on an appropriate occasion, to the consideration of debriefing itself.)
8. It is useful to draw out the learner's perceptions of the teacher's motives (or these motives of whoever set up the practical experience). It is fruitful to compare various replies and share your own and/or those of the initiator of the experience.
9. Focusing upon the educational *ends* of the action and the theories which informed it is also helpful. Perhaps a distinction can be drawn between learning from practice and learning through practice.
10. It is important to focus on where the learner can turn to compare with others her experiences, reflections, and theorising. (This will include other known learners, the writings of theorists, other people present at the same practical situation.)

(These principles were first published in Fish, 1988.)

In all of this, of course, the ultimate aim is to get the *learner* to raise these kinds of question for herself and with herself as part of her own reflections upon *any* practice in which she is engaged. Thus, such debriefing will work towards encouraging autonomous reflection in action.

Deliberation (or practical reasoning)

Deliberation is the activity that Schwab was concerned to substitute for what he saw as the overtheoretical and moribund approach of earlier curriculum studies. Basically, it is concerned with making curriculum decisions, usually about the design, implementation or evaluation of curriculum, and usually (though not necessarily) on a larger scale than the teaching and learning decisions made by an individual within one classroom. It is *not*, however, as in the popular view, simply a discussion with colleagues about plans. It involves: 'weighing and examining the reasons for and against a measure and giving careful consideration and mature reflection to the choices available' (Harris, 1986, p.18). This, then, is a vital aspect of learning through practice, since it enables the student to consider the broader implications of personal theory, as it develops.

For Schwab, deliberation is a process of curriculum planning on a large scale by decision-making in small groups. He argues that the three processes of deliberation are discovery, coalescence, and utilisation. The various stages of discovery of how the issue is seen at a personal and group level are followed by a coalescence of the group's aims, data and judgement, and this leads to knowledge which is used creatively to produce the curriculum design. Schwab thinks that up to ten meetings may be necessary to establish the base for taking decisions (Schwab, 1978).

As Reid points out, however, deliberation is in its purest form where there is consciousness of the need to justify decisions in general terms, and where group members are in sufficiently prolonged contact to be able to engage in the discovery process (Reid, 1978). In initial training, the group might consist of the teacher, tutor and student.

For tutors who have been redesigning courses for the CNAA and other bodies, and for teachers in school working on curriculum initiatives, deliberation is a very familiar process. In a first post the new teacher will be expected to contribute to this process in planning teams, as well as to demonstrate it in her own planning. Experience of this for the student might be gained as part of a three-cornered conversation about lessons or a scheme of work with a tutor and a teacher and by observing planning teams on placement during training.

But a danger note must also be sounded about all of this. While the intentions of and the results of deliberation are clear and are already with us in less systematic form, there are some doubts about the processes that Schwab has proposed. There is little sound evidence of how this more systematic approach actually works in schools, and there are, it is argued, barriers to successful deliberation. (See, for example, Pereira, 1984; Knitter, 1985; Roby, 1986; and Harris, 1986.)

These issues lead to questions about the designing of the initial training course itself.

6. Developing a Curriculum for Initial Training: Some Design Issues

Summary

- Three models of course design
  - the product model
  - the process model
  - the research model
- Seven key issues
  - what kind of teachers do we want?
  - what is involved in teaching?
  - what is involved in learning to teach?
  - what is the relationship of initial training to in-service education?
  - some recent trends
  - the requirements of the accreditors
  - who will be the candidates for training?
- course design for initial training
  - content
  - structure and sequence
  - the role of tutor and teacher
  - the role of college and school
  - assessment and monitoring
- Two kinds of model for initial training
  - some models for learning through practice
  - four models for relating theory to practice

Introduction

The intention of this chapter is to rehearse some issues which have to be faced whenever a new course for, or a new approach to, initial training has to be developed, and thus to establish some common knowledge about the design of training leading to Qualified Teacher Status (QTS). The underlying intentions are to lay bare the essentially problematic nature of the issues, an understanding of which will be necessary whatever the ultimate form of training. For this reason, the terms 'course' and 'student' have been used below, but the principles also apply to any form of training leading to QTS.

Three models of course design

The real significance of course design in teacher training, which does not apply in any other area, is the double-faceted nature of the operation. Designers in this field are *both* designing course content from which students will learn, *and* designing methods and providing a model of design from which students will also learn. They will, properly, be learners of teaching and of educational course construction through both what is offered to them, and how it is offered.

With this in mind, it is useful to remind ourselves of three major models of course design derived from Stenhouse (1975). While they are not the only models in existence, they do represent three which are common in course construction for many forms of professional training. They are:

The product model (also known as the objectives model and the transmission model)
The process model
The research model.

Only a very brief description and critique of each can be offered here.

The product model

This model of course design is based on the assumptions of behavioural psychology, that learning can be defined as a visible and measurable change in behaviour, and that the basic unit of such learning is 'conditioning' (ie, the attachment of a response to a previously neutral stimulus).

To devise a curriculum based on this model requires the designer to describe the intentions of the course in terms of behavioural objectives which must:

- describe the change in the learner in terms of measurable behaviour
- involve sharply specified goal behaviour
- ensure that such goals are measureable (and therefore visible in some way)
- ensure that these goals are specified unambiguously
- see these objectives as forming the basis of the instructions to be given to the learners.

The whole approach is open to all the familiar charges levelled at behaviourism. It provides an inadequate concept of education, learning, and instruction, and it begs many questions about the principles of selection of what is to be learnt. It leads to inflexible programmes, which cannot take on board individual differences, and erodes the teacher's opportunities for ongoing creativity while teaching. And it presupposes that all subjects work in the same way. In other words, it disrupts the integrity of learning, and does not respect the individualism of learner, teacher or content. Further, clear behavioural objectives have proved very difficult to write for anything but the most trivial aspects of learning. (See MacDonald-Ross, 1975, and Clark, 1979.)

The process model

This model is best described in relation to the above model, as Table 1 shows.

Table 1: *The process and product model*

The Product Model	The Process Model
A transmission of knowledge model	An heuristic model
Stresses knowledge and skills, concepts and criteria	Stresses understanding and procedures
Content is 'given'	All is negotiated
Student activities involve absorbing, note-taking, remembering	Student activities involve experiencing and reflecting
Student is passive studier	Student is investigator, explorer
Motivation is via content, teacher activity	Motivation is via involvement
Discourages creative thinking	Encourages creative thinking
Sees student as one of a class	Sees student as individual
Is teacher-centred	Is student-centred
Sees teacher as expert, examiner	Sees teacher as learner, explorer, critic, developer, resource
Does not encourage student autonomy	Does encourage student autonomy
Teacher often works with class alone	Teacher often works with a team
Sees teaching as technical-rational activity, clear-cut, efficient	Sees teaching as artistic activity, tentative, open to challenge and change
Sees teacher as pursuing marks	Sees teacher as pursuing understanding
Sees assessment as simple, end of course product	Sees assessment as ongoing part of learning
Defines education as training in knowledge	Finds definition of education problematic
Defines knowledge as indisputable, permanent and propositional	Defines knowledge as relative, temporary, procedural
Mistakes, by simplifying, the nature of knowledge and learning	Wants to include in knowledge experience plus reflection on it
Thinks the relationship between theory and practice is simple	Sees the relationship of theory and practice as problematic, complex
Readily analyses content, aims, into specific simple objectives	Can specify aims, but refers then to principles of procedure
Uses short, clear-cut time blocks	Needs flexibility of time
'Covers content' efficiently (perhaps at expense of understanding)	Covers less ground but enables better assimilation, greater motivation
Uses fewer and simpler resources	Is heavily resource-based

Developing a Curriculum for Initial Training 89

In the process model, everything is directed at improving the processes of learning, and even assessment plays a central role in this. Instead of appearing at the end of the learning process, merely as a check on the success, it becomes a part of the process, appearing at all points during the programme, and is thus used to feed back helpful information to the student as she goes along. This also has a major significance for attendance patterns. The contact sessions offered in the process model are designed to offer vital processes and experiences instead of which no amount of reading or note-copying would be a proper substitute. Student attendance at a process course has therefore to be more extensive than at a course based on the transmission model.

By comparison, the research model takes a rather different view.

The research model

If we accept that we do not always know in advance the answers to education questions, nor exactly where we wish the learners to end up, nor whether the policies we currently hold will evolve and adapt to new conditions, then we may see as appropriate a more experimental approach, both to the planning of the curriculum and to the learning in progress within it. The focus here would, then, be upon the problems to address, rather than an agenda of issues to be mastered.

This notion as the basis of curriculum planning might well have an attraction for teacher training where, arguably, apart from some very basic matters, there are few techniques and strategies of teaching commonly agreed as essential. There are simply too many variables involved in the enterprise of education for students to be safe in learning any set repertoire of strategies. What they may need instead is the means of devising their own decisions and approaches as they go along.

The presentation of such a course on paper would probably be very similar to that for the process model, specifying intentions, principles of procedure and adding perhaps more detail on the problems to be addressed, and the roles of the teacher and learner. In general, the role of the teacher (tutor, in this case) would need to be more recessive than that adopted in the process model, and more committed to genuine exploration. The real exploration for the tutor might most usefully be that of exploring how the learners are exploring the problematic issues. This casts the teachers and the learners in a parallel rather than in an identical enquiry role.

Broadly, then, the point about the research model is that, for teacher training, it involves three levels of enquiry:

(a) pupils in the classroom researching or investigating issues at their own level. (The word 'researching' here is used to mean looking at issues to which there is no one specific answer, so that neither the pupil nor the initiating teacher knows beforehand all of what might be discovered. By comparison, 'investigation' implies that the teacher at least knows the range of possible outcomes for which the pupil is searching.)

(b) student teachers in the classroom researching or investigating their own teaching and their pupils' learning
(c) the tutor researching his own teaching and his students' learning.

There are many possibilities here which might make this very attractive to the trainers. But there are two preconditions without which this model could lead to failure. There is a need for a commitment on the part of all involved to experimentation, which is against the government's present mood about education and particularly teacher education. And there is a need to see the issues of teaching and teacher education as essentially problematic. This is also currently against the trend of government publications in which a generally more simplistic view is taken of teaching and teacher training.

Seven key issues

This section seeks to address seven questions which would have to be faced by a curriculum developer before detailed planning for an initial training course could be started. They are addressed in terms of questions on a bipolar model. The intention here is simply to offer examples of the kinds of argument which have to be addressed, as a means of fuelling deliberation about these matters.

What kind of teachers do we want?

This issue immediately confronts us with the problems associated with the value-based nature of educational concepts. It also raises the issue of who is 'we' in this question, and who has the right to try to answer it anyway?

- has everyone who is involved in education?
- have only the clients of initial training? (who are they?)
- does everyone who teaches know about how to train a teacher?
- should only the government and the validating bodies determine what is offered?

Already it is beginning to emerge that the whole business is complex. To return, then, to the original question: broadly, what kind of teacher do we want?

- a conservative teacher who will fit the present profession or a radical teacher who will seek to change things as he goes along?
- a narrow specialist in terms of both subject and age-range, or one trained on a broad base?
- an expert in content or in professional artistry?
- one who can do only as he has been told, or one who has the confidence to experiment and thus to go on learning?
- one who relies on intuition alone and continues to repeat a narrow set of experiences, or one who, by analysis of intuition and practice, develops insight?

There will always be considerable debate about the longer-term goals of initial training. But as if this set of interrelated questions were not enough, there are also other issues to be resolved.

What is involved in teaching?

There are, of course, as many answers to this as there are answerers. In addition to the approach indicated above in Chapter 3, which asks whether teaching is an artistic or a scientific activity, there are many other approaches. A useful text in this respect is John Passmore's *The Philosophy of Teaching*. He details the skills, capacities, habits, dispositions, abilities and knowledge that are part of teaching. His work is an important antidote to the idea currently prevalent that teaching is a matter of learning a few simple skills and strategies.

What is involved in learning to teach?

Here we have two key issues: what kind of things do we need to learn in order to learn to teach? and: What might we do in order to learn them?

Contrary to the untutored view of many of the public, learning to teach involves learning far more than the skills of classroom management. Trainees need to learn about themselves, about their various capacities for relating to and fostering the learning of other people, their knowledge of their subject, of children and their development, and a clear understanding of various theoretical perspectives, together with an ability to form their own personal theory.

What is the relationship of initial training to in-service education?

This is another difficult issue. Every time changes are promised to in-service work and the arrangements for the probationary year, this affects the thinking about the intentions for all teacher education courses. For example, if initial training really is only the start of a compulsory longer period of education for teachers, and if all were to have a fully supervised probation, and to be required to complete in-service courses, then initial training might confine itself to elucidating and then fostering a foundation for later training. Given present circumstances, then, what kind of contribution should the initial training course make to teacher education?

- should it produce the fully fledged and fully equipped teacher or, given GRIST opportunities, should it only produce a trainee who is merely ready to learn the proper job?
- what should the balance be between the time devoted to the subject knowledge that teachers will need in the classroom, that devoted to gaining practical teaching competences, and that aimed at the deeper issues of education?
- what should the balance be between theory and practice, and how should the practical training interrelate with theory?
- should it offer only the basic pedagogical skills or a wide range of

perspectives on classrooms and schools?
- should it offer complex curriculum theory and a sophisticated understanding of how schools work and are related to the outside world, or simply focus on the delivery of the National Curriculum?
- how much should be made of the current bandwagons in education?
- should it be reactive to present schooling or proactive in looking to future developments?

But while these matters wax and wane in fashion, there are also other trends which need to be noted.

Some recent trends

There are three trends which during the 1980s have exerted an influence upon the development of initial training courses. They are:

1. the role of school-based work
2. the role of teachers as supervisors of teaching practice
3. whether work in education itself is as personally educative as work in traditional academic subjects.

Issues about the value of school-based work have recently influenced course development very considerably, and the government and the validating bodies have been demanding more of it. Yet the strengths and weaknesses of locating more of the course within schools seem not to have been as clearly debated as they might. This is in spite of the fact that a number of training institutions have school-based work as 50 per cent of their course. In the absence of a report from the Cambridge research on school-based courses, and of other clear analysis of these issues, as yet unfounded assumptions have been growing that the more the course is based in school the better. But it is the nature of the course that really matters, not its location.

Issues about partnership in teacher training have led particularly to questions about the exact role of teachers as supervisors of teaching practice. Again, there is little clear evidence of the pros and cons of this idea. But it is an issue which course development teams will need to consider.

Thorny and interrelated issues about the content of training courses are currently influencing course development. They have arisen as a result of the government requirements that training for the BEd student should contain two years of main subject study at undergraduate level. Some trainers see this as a return to the kind of training offered in the 1960s. Whether this is a return to previous approaches or not, of course, the real question is whether it is a better way of preparing the student for teaching. The significant issues, therefore, are whether:

- the study of education practice and theory is as personally educative and enriching as traditional academic subjects
- the study of main subjects at the student's own level is just as practically effective as the study of education in preparing teachers to work

Developing a Curriculum for Initial Training 93

in classrooms
- whether academic work is as professionally significant as work directly relevant to the classroom.

But if these are the fashionable trends to be considered by course developers, there are also a number of absolute requirements made of them by the government.

The requirements of the accreditors

The government, as the accreditors of all initial training courses, have made some very clear demands about the content of initial training.

There are two main sources from which we can learn about these. They are, directly, via the documentation on initial training, and indirectly, via the documentation about the probationary year.

The key documents which deal directly with initial training have mostly already been referred to in Chapter 2. However, in that chapter there was no detail given of the specific content requirements, and so it is necessary to record them here.

The most revealing documents are two HMI discussion papers previously cited (*Teacher Training in the Secondary School*, DES, January 1981; and *Teaching in Schools: The Content of Initial Training*, DES, 1983a), and *CATENOTES* 3 and 4, which made their ideas mandatory. They appeared from the end of 1981 onwards.

From *Teacher Training in the Secondary School* we learn that:
- students need to be introduced to the whole view of the curriculum and the language and thought of curriculum theory (pp.4–11)
- they must give more consideration to pupils' social and personal development (pp.13–14)
- they should be aware of the role of assessment as an integral part of the teaching process (pp.14–15)
- they must take more account of the needs of the less able (pp.15–16).

As a base for further discussion about the objectives of initial training the paper then offers a three-stage model of the professional development of the teacher. (These stages are: the first year of teaching; two or three years' experience; and, finally, the stage where the teacher is taking 'advanced responsibility' (p.17).) It then continues, encouragingly, and in a tone lost in later papers:

> most teacher trainers would probably agree that the broad aim of initial training is to prepare teachers for schools as they are and at the same time to equip them to be agents of change.
>
> The former puts a premium upon the building up of knowledge and initial confidence, and the latter upon the acquiring of criteria for educational judgements . . . The growth of confidence during intial training is an uncerain business, but its best chance lies in frequent and well regulated contacts with children and schools and the gradual mastery of a number of skills and competencies. Identify-

ing these and keeping them under review is a responsiblity of college staffs and validators. (DES, 1981, pp.17–18)

From his earliest days the student should be encouraged to develop as a theorist in his own right or he may reject theory in favour of the rigidly practical, and lose the insights that go with it. (DES, 1981, p.18)

Unfortunately, once these ideas had hardened into requirements their sublety was lost. From *Teaching in Schools: The Content of Initial Training* came 20 recommendations, which were turned into criteria for accreditation by *CATENOTE 4*. The following demands are the most important for course developers. Numbers refer to clauses in *Teaching in Schools*.

1. A minimum of two years equivalent should be given to subject study in the four-year BEd, primary and secondary (presumably in preparation for the National Curriculum).
2. There shall be an agreed minimum range of professional content.
8. A substantial period of time must be spent in studying the methodology of teaching subject or subjects.
9. Professional studies for all primary and middle years' teachers should include the study of children's development in language and mathematics, based on the recommendations of government reports.
11. All courses must include some means of understanding children's learning and development; the place of education in society; and ways in which the background of pupils influences their learning potential.
12. Partnership between schools and initial training institutions should be strengthened at all levels, and in all aspects.
13. Students on PGCE courses should spend at least 12 weeks and preferably more full time in schools, while those on BEd four-year courses should spend 20 weeks minimum.
14. All courses should include:
    practical experience and knowledge of class management and control: knowledge of . . . the full range of pupils in terms of ability, behaviour, social background and culture: experience and knowledge of the level of performance appropriate for children of differing ages, abilities and backgrounds: awareness of the ethical, spiritual and aesthetic values of society as well as the democratic and economic foundations on which it is based: respect for and understanding of the wide cultural heritage which belongs to children growing up in our society.
15. Students' main teaching subjects should be tutored by staff with a high ability in those subjects, so that students' curiosity and enjoyment is stimulated. Links should be made with the subject outside the classroom, in the everyday life and work of the community.
16. The professional aspects of courses should be taught by staff who are successful and experienced and up-to-date members of the teaching profession, who can communicate their knowledge to the students.
17. Courses should be based on 'guided study and experiment, and therefore under-taught rather than over-taught'.

18. They should be taught in order to encourage 'commitment to continuous professional learning and intellectual renewal throughout their careers'. (DES, 1983a, pp. 16–18)

But it is three government documents on the probationary year that illustrate the real focus on specific pedagogical skills. They perhaps reveal that aspect of initial training that the government really wants to promote. Not surprisingly, what is emphasised here is that part of teaching which is most easily monitored, appraised, and measured. The three documents are: *The New Teacher in School*, DES (1982), *Administrative Memorandum 1/83: The Treatment and Assessment of Probationary Teachers*, DES, January 26 (1983b) and *The New Teacher in School*, DES (1988b).

Of these three documents, it is the Memorandum which comes more succinctly to the point. Under section 6, assistance for probationers from school and LEA staff, the document lists the need for comparable and equitable arrangements for assessment of all probationers, and adds, interestingly:

> Probationers should be aware of the criteria on which they will be assessed; these should include *class management, relevant subject expertise, appropriate teaching skills, adequacy of lesson preparation, use of resources, understanding the needs of the pupils, ability to establish appropriate relationships with pupils and colleagues,* (DES, 1983b, p.4, section 6d, italics mine)

Here, then, at last we have the real agenda for the full entry to the profession. Interestingly, this information was not readily available to either the student or the initial trainers, except through the usual HMSO publication form for Circulars and Administrative Memoranda until part of it was republished in 1988 as Appendix 3 to *The New Teacher in School (DES, 1988b)*. *The New Teacher in School (1982)* also covertly indicated this same basic and narrow agenda for the probationary year.

This document, based on the notion of the mastery of teaching skills, reports and comments upon a survey of 588 lessons given by probationers in primary and secondary schools. Probationers were marked on a five-point scale across three lessons each, and were observed for 12 pre-specified categories:

- relationships with pupils
- classroom management
- the planning and preparation of work
- the level of stimulation of the presentation
- aims and objectives
- assessment
- the choice of materials
- links with previous work
- the achievement of aims
- the match of work to pupils
- awareness of the mixed ability, special needs, multi-ethnic demands
- the quality of language in the classroom (useful dialogues; pupils

encouraged to express own ideas; pupils' language suitably extended; teacher's language, questions and answers).

Here, then, we have the real detail of what counts as important for the new teacher.* But if this is what is required by HMI of the probationer, course developers also need to take account of who the candidates for training are and what they bring to the training.

Who will be the candidates for training?

What is important to bear in mind here is that until the mid 1980s there have been mainly two kinds of candidates for initial training, the BEd student (too often straight from school), and the graduate. But initial training in the late 1980s is going through two major upheavals in respect of this. First, by the early 1990s there will be a phenomenal shortfall of 18 year olds, and so many institutions are now gearing up for large numbers of mature students, most of whom will enter training on non-standard entry qualifications or will come on to training courses from special Access Courses (courses designed to offer mature students without standard A level qualifications a means of obtaining them or their equivalent). This raises vast issues about the kind of training required by experienced students with non-traditional academic backgrounds. Second, in 1992, under new European Economic Community rules, there will be a whole new market of untrained graduates from a range of European countries, who may well enter teaching in Britain under licence and gain their training via a kind of sandwich course arrangement, according to how the school and the LEA see their needs. This is likely to raise major issues. In both cases, clearly, the trainees' starting points in terms of knowledge and maturity need to be taken into account by course developers.

Having considered some external and internal influences on initial training, what can we now say about the design of courses?

Course design for initial training

Content

The following questions demonstrate the complexity of this notion for those planning from scratch.

How can we determine what should be the major components of training?

- by looking at what a 'good' teacher is and can do?
- by looking at what society/schools/parents/pupils want now from a teacher?
- by looking at how to divide up educational, professional, and academic knowledge?
- by going only for what will suit the short-term aims?
- by looking at where the students start, and asking what they need in order to make progress?

---

* See page 197.

Developing a Curriculum for Initial Training 97

- by going only for the most commonly expressed characteristics?
- by defining the long-term goals for training in terms of the kind of teachers we want?

This leads us back again to the question faced earlier: who has the right to say?

When it comes to the structure of the course, the most basic components are those associated with theory and practice. This takes us back to the issues raised in Chapters 4 and 5.

Structure and sequence

What is the role of practice and theory? The following are some of the key questions:

- what practical expertise can and should we offer a beginning teacher?
- what theoretical perspectives should we offer?
- what is the distinction between formal theory and personal theory?
- what kinds of practical experience must students have before they qualify as teachers?
- how can we offer these experiences?
- how can we help students to develop their own personal theory?
- how can we foster learning from practice?
- what kinds of practice are now available for students?

These issues prompt a further question:

What is the role of college-based and school-based work?

The following are some of the questions which might enable planners to think about the siting of courses:

- what exactly can be learnt in school rather than college?
- what exactly can be better learnt in college rather than school?
- are there any advantages in being able to discuss some matters outside the school?
- what might be the benefits and the disadvantages for the college and the school in shifting the entire training to the school premises?

This takes us back to issues about the bases of partnership, and the role of the partners.

The role of tutor and teacher

In addition to the issues raised above, the following questions may help to clarify their respective contributions. Not only can they be asked of the individuals who will be involved in the individual course, but they can also be asked of the jobs of teaching and tutoring themselves:

- what are the differences in the perspectives of the two jobs?
- what kinds of experience do they require?

- what kinds of expertise do they require?
- what aims might each have in preparing students to teach?
- are their responsibilities to the pupils the same?
- are their responsibilities to the students the same?
- do they share the same theoretical knowledge?
- do they have the same view of how you learn to teach?

The most important question which follows these is: how can their similarities and differences best be harnessed in the training enterprise?

The role of college and school

This question opens up all of the issues about the resourcing of training, particularly in the present climate. The issue must, however, be confronted by the planners in spite of the fact that the government currently seems to assume that the new approaches to training will not raise such questions. There is a need to work towards a clearer idea of these roles, not at an administrative level, but at an educational one.

Perhaps this is one area in which schools should be wary, since individual teachers on local CATE courses are now committing their colleagues to a partnership which might require considerable additional resources in the next few years.

Assessment and monitoring

Broadly, there are two kinds of assessment implications to be considered in planning initial training. They are:

1. What kinds of assessment will help students learn to teach?
2. How is responsibility for assessment going to be divided between the partners in initial training?

In both cases there are significant issues to be raised. The first question has never yet been satisfactorily answered. Of course, the most logical form of assessing the *success* of the student as a teacher on any particular occasion would be to assess the progress in learning of her pupils. But nothing will avoid the problems of the subjectivity of assessment. Further, it does not test the issues which are more vital in the long term – the question of how to use assessment to *assist* the student to learn to teach. And how to assess the fitness of the student to enter the teaching profession. The second question is going to be no less problematic whatever the details of partnership and of training in the 1990s.

Some further issues about assessment are looked at in Chapter 12.

Two kinds of model for initial training

Some models for learning through practice

The following seven models for learning through practice might be of use in determining the kinds of strategy to be used on the practical side of the students' work.

Sitting with Nellie
This is the apprenticeship model taken from industry in which the novice sat beside the factory worker and learnt the job from observation and copying. This might be characterised by the phrase: 'Just model yourself on me dear.' This captures the dangers of importing such a model into learning to teach, where *people* rather than things are the product, and therefore where the job is unpredictable and personal.

Pure observation
This equally simplistic model assumes that teaching is the same activity for everyone and that its central characteristics are visible to the observer, and learnable by copying. This is characterised by the phrase: 'See how it's done by watching.' This is a behaviourist approach and assumes that teaching is all about performance.

Total immersion
This model implies that the only way to learn to teach is to be plunged into the most difficult activity and either to learn to survive or be quickly seen as a failure. The phrase that sums up this attitude is: 'We'll give her 4Z and see if she survives.' The assumptions here are that no one can learn to teach, that it is a matter of instinct for survival, and that this instinct will always be sound if it holds up on one occasion.

Task analysis
This model is based upon the notion that teaching is a skill-based activity and that the teacher should begin by analysing the task to be learnt. Thus, for this model, to learn to teach is merely a matter of learning to analyse the learner's task. This is best characterised by the question: 'How many sub-skills in running for the door?' Again, the underlying assumptions are behaviourist.

Micro-teaching
This model of learning to teach assumes that teaching can be learnt by operating on a small scale in a sheltered situation, usually with a video camera running, and then analysing that teaching with a view to improving it next time. It does not take account of the interrelationship of theory and practice in practice as discussed in Chapter 5. It might be summed up in the phrase: 'When I saw myself I nearly died.'

Group instructional practice
This model of learning to teach assumes that a whole group of students can learn from watching or working with a tutor in a school classroom. The following phrase sums this up: 'One tutor, five students and 23 pupils means a ration of 1 to 4, thank God.'

Double Focus technique
This model of learning to teach involves the notion that a teacher, a tutor, a group of students, and a class of pupils can all be involved in both teaching and learning from each other in the normal school classroom. (See Chapter 10 for details.) The Double Focus here refers to the duality of teaching and learning to teach simultaneously.

If these models are about learning to teach, the following are about relating theory to practice.

Four models for relating theory to practice

David Webb and Michael Wilkinson have developed four models which broadly sum up the relationship of theory to practice in initial training courses. These are:

> *The separatist model.* Here theory and practice are seen as two separate, significant but not essentially interconnected, strands of the course.
> *The coincidental model.* Here theory offers a background for practice rather than anything of direct relevance to the classroom. Any relevance that emerges is held as purely coincidental. There is no consideration here that practice might inform theory.
> *The relationist model.* Here theory and practice are closely related. It is believed that a body of theory relevant to the classroom exists and that it can have a direct influence upon what happens there. Current practice is seen here to illustrate theory.
> *The individualist model.* This model assumes that the only relevant theory for any individual practitioner in the classroom is that derived from his personal experience. This involves the close analysis of a range of experiences by and with the help of a range of professionals. It is also part of this thinking that practice can modify theory.
>
> (Webb and Wilkinson, 1980)

In many ways their four-part model neatly summarises much of the thinking presented in both this chapter and Chapter 5. It does not, however, take account of a fifth approach which derives personal theory from practice by drawing on both formal thory and the help of professionals in the analysis of practice.

If there, then, are the theoretical design issues to be considered at the planning stage, how might this planning work out in practice?

Part 2

Partnership in Practice: Intermittent School Experience

7. Some Basic Moves Towards Partnership: Observation Reconsidered

Summary

- Observation: the practice and some theory
  - the technique and its rationale
  - four levels of observation
  - the purposes of observation in detail
  - the techniques of observation
- Observation: some examples
  - pre-course observation
  - day visits
- Student perspectives
  - first reactions
  - some critical insights
  - some sharp words
- Reflections upon observation
  - the place of reflection and deliberation
  - the role of the teacher and the tutor
  - the place of observation in the course as a whole
- The practical implications
  - for teachers
  - for tutors
  - for students

Introduction

There are many versions of school experience in which a teacher teaches a class of pupils in their normal school setting, observed by one or even two students, who then reflect (or not) upon what has been seen. This basic pattern occurs so commonly that it appears in one form or another in almost every kind of initial training course and many teachers in both primary and secondary schools are involved in this way of working.

However, the practical implications of and the theoretical rationale for this work have not always been fully thought through, either by schools and colleges or by teachers and tutors. This chapter seeks to provide a basis from which observation might be reconsidered in terms of both partnership and reflective techniques.

Observation: the practice and some theory

The technique and its rationale

By contrast with the version of school experience described in the chapters which follow, the strategy for intermittent experience described here is well known, frequently used, and simple. Indeed, in some versions, it might be said to be rather too simple in its conception and implementation.

At best, intermittent school experience can provide the central thrust for a whole training programme, and a number of institutions use it in this way (though what happens in detail has sometimes been left to little more than chance). Certainly, too, in many cases, intermittent experience can provide an arena for real experimentation.

At worst, however, such observation visits can deteriorate into desultory days in a variety of schools on a very fragmented programme, with up to 90 students being sent out in threes, fours or even sixes, to up to 30 schools to sit with teachers in their classrooms and to explore the school. Given the scale and the six or so tutors involved, there can be little detailed coordination of this work either across or within schools. This can mean that there is almost no immediately relevant preparation by the tutor, who cannot be present during the visit itself (for logistical reasons), but who, somehow, has to field any follow-up. Students often do not know what to look for in classrooms, and cannot always see what they are looking at. It certainly means latent frustration for the teachers involved, who often neither receive nor contribute to any evaluation and deliberation, and who, despite shouldering most of the responsibilities *in situ*, have no idea what the students either have or should have learnt from their experience in school, nor of how it relates to the rest of the training course.

This technique might be caricatured as 'observing the teacher, class or group, but talking to tutor'. Its rationale (where one has been articulated at all) has had much more to do with the numbers game in terms of staff-student ratios (because it is tutor labour-saving) than to do with views on the best ways in which students can learn.

Of itself, the basic strategy of 'observing' a teacher and a class might or might not be a useful tool in learning to teach. It is what is involved in the activity of observation, the quality of the observations, and the short- and long-term uses to which these are put by the student, which affect the quality of the training and ultimately, possibly, the quality of the student's teaching. The activity of observation might or might not involve extensive interaction with pupils, but the observation techniques used should be subservient to the ends for which the observation is carried out. Those ends should involve learning through practice (as opposed to *from* it). Thus, the activity is not about teacher appraisal or pupil assessment, but about reflecting upon and deliberating about the practice in order to understand it better. Once this end is established and the specific situation for observation has been selected, the choice of technique will follow.

Thus, observation might be best embedded in a complex pattern of work, for which the tutor, teacher, and students have together prepared. The preparation would include tutor and teacher sharing perceptions about observation; tutor and students preparing together in terms of what will be involved in the observation and the specific contextual details of it; and student and teacher establishing a basis for observation and reflection upon it. (Some parts of this would take longer than others, and some, like the teacher and tutor sharing, might involve a once-for-all agreement of a basic working framework which is then only 'topped up' by brief conference about current details.) After the observation there would be a full debriefing. Then the learning sequence for the student becomes that of:

- preparing with tutor and with teacher (refining and clarifying the nature of the tasks)
- observing practice (with a view to learning through not from it)
- reflecting on this, both during the observation, and afterwards
- learning by drawing principles from this, and by reading about the issues
- making resolutions for later practice, later observation, investigation or teaching.

Four levels of observation

Observation, then, is not watching in order to copy, but in order to refine one's *own* thinking and ultimately one's own actions. Without knowledge of how to observe, analyse or consider critically what has been seen, learning and refining will not occur.

Learning by observing, with a view to reflection about and deliberation upon what is being or has been seen, can contribute to learning to teach at four levels.

- It can help to shape in the student's mind what can and what should (and should not) be done.
- It can help her to begin to consider whether and/or how she personally can operate within a classroom.
- It can begin the vital process of associating action with reflection and deliberation – before, during, and after action – which can help the student to develop her own personal theory.
- Properly embedded in other school experience activities (see Chapters 8, 9, 10), it can help the student to see how a wide variety of practical experience, together with a range of theoretical perspectives, can contribute to personal theory.

A key to this kind of learning, then, lies in the handling of both the observation on the one hand, and the debriefing, reflection, and deliberation on the other. And it is hard to see how these vitally related activities can actually come together to make sense at all if the teacher is the focus and moving force of the one, and the tutor is the enabler of the other. For this reason what is needed is an observation programme which is in all respects jointly organised in detail by tutor and teacher together, and fewer schools which each take more students and one tutor.

The purposes of observation in detail

Within the broad intention that all observation is dedicated to helping the student to refine her own thinking rather than to copy blindly what has been seen, there is a need for the partners to clarify the purpose of observation on every occasion on which it is employed. They will also need to draw on a joint understanding of the place of the observation work within the course as a whole.

An essential issue which is frequently neglected is the need during early planning to be precise about the intentions and the procedures of the reflection sessions. Paradoxically, this is especially so when the post-observation reflection session will include or will be wholly concerned with the unexpected events of the lesson. Here, careful joint preparation between teacher and tutor needs to take account of what is likely to emerge, how to keep the observation widely yet sharply focused, how to get the students to document it, and how to organise relevant subsequent reflections.

In other words, the activities to be observed (whether set up by tutor or by teacher) should be planned as a practicum. It is systematic observation which fosters learning through practice, and not the *ad hoc* attempt, during a hastily pulled together debriefing, to make something of an unplanned and even irrelevant experience, which is unrelated to the intended task but which the unlucky student has just encountered in a busy school which has made no more than general preparations for the day's visit. Observation is not, as some still seem to think, necessarily good or useful no matter what is observed. But such a practicum, though it needs to provide carefully orchestrated observations, should not be seen as an attempt to strait-jacket the school. Rather it should be a joint venture worked out together by tutor and teacher in order to suit students and pupils. The practical implications of this are discussed below.

The techniques of observation

It follows from this that the particular technique(s) of observation used should be chosen to suit the purpose of observation and should come from the whole range of such techniques. Their selection should be made in the light of knowledge of:

- the possibilities of the techniques chosen, and their limitations (including issues of interpretation and recording)
- the value of debriefing as part of the learning process
- the importance of the students' reflections
- the problems involved in learning a practical activity
- the problems of designing training courses and techniques.

Observation: some examples

Pre-course observation

Issues about the possible focus and specificity of any written guides to observation for the students might best be raised by considering the following fictional example designed to help them on the pre-course experience required of students either in the summer or the September before their course begins.

Figure 1 below is designed for use in a two-week period of pre-course experience, which students would normally be required to complete in a school of their choice. The same range of consideration might be expected of students irrespective of their intended subject or age-range specialisation.

Pre-course Experience
It is intended that this experience will provide:

(a) a clearer insight into the range of skills, capacities, knowledge, and roles that are part of being a teacher

(b) an opportunity to observe, meet, and talk to pupils of the widely differing ages and abilities to be found across the full range of the school (primary or secondary)

(c) an opportunity to hear the views of the full range of adults associated with the school

(d) some awareness of current practice in primary/secondary education

(e) what can be involved in the activities of observation, interpretation, recording, and appraisal.

Some of the following procedures may help towards these intentions. You should discuss this sheet with a relevant senior member of staff before you begin.

EXPECT TO SHARE WITH THE SCHOOL ANYTHING YOU WRITE DOWN

---

1. Take as many opportunities as possible to involve yourself in the full life of the school, and seek to meet pupils in a wide variety of differing situations (in break-times, in out-of-class activities, in registration groups and assemblies as well as in classrooms, the gym/hall, and playing fields).
    From observations and talking to a range of pupils note:
    – their interests, enthusiasms, and abilities, both in and out of class
    – how these change in different age-groups
    – how they respond in different groupings in class.

2. Try to see a wide range of classes (if secondary, in your own subject areas) with differing ages, abilities, and groupings.

From observation and by analysis, note:
- the organisation of subject material and resources and how this affects learning
- the organisation of pupils and how this affects learning
- provision for, and the differing abilities of, high and low attainers.

3. By arrangement, follow one pupil designated to you by the school across two school days. Do this by following the class or group that pupil is in. (**NB: DO NOT DRAW THE PUPIL'S ATTENTION TO WHAT YOU ARE DOING**).

    From your observation of and discussions with this pupil among others, note:
    - the varying demands made on him/her in different contexts in one day
    - the differing skills and abilities s/he has to call upon in different contexts during one day.

4. If possible, arrange to follow a teacher (if secondary, of your subject) for one whole school day – including registration periods, administrative requirements, and work in any non-lesson periods.

    From observations and talking to him/her note:
    - the varying demands made on him/her in different contexts during one day
    - the skills, capacities, abilities, strategies, knowledge s/he is required to demonstrate.

5. As a result of your general impressions from classroom and staffroom, playground and corridor, try to jot down what seem to you to be the key priorities of schooling in practice, and the key issues currently under discussion.

6. Collect all available published material from the school, including all documents given to staff and pupils and sent to parents. What conclusions do you come to and what impressions do you have of the school's aims and priorities?

7. Talk to as many staff as possible, including the headteacher and non-teaching members, about the school's aims and priorities.

8. If possible, attend a meeting involving parents.

Figure 1: Pre-course experience

Although Figure 1 shows a fictional observation sheet it raises issues about what such sheets might contain; about observation techniques and the recording and use of data; about the implications for pupils, parents, and the school; and about how students might be drawn to learn through this.

Students would normally be required to make notes (which would be open to the school) as part of any exercise. Such note-making, if deliberative rather than factual, can become the beginning of the reflection process. That process, if applied to pre-course observation, can then be drawn upon and extended when the students begin their course. The experiences can

Some Basic Moves Towards Partnership

then begin to be turned into learning and into a means of encouraging the student to construct an agenda of her own priorities for the training course. One means of achieving this is by a questionnaire which asks for details of the experience, the classes met, the work carried out, the insights gained, the problems encountered, and what is now hoped for from the course. This data can be linked to discussion of definitions of education, of what schools should be and are attempting to achieve, of ways of organising pupils' learning, of multicultural and equal opportunities issues, of what influences the marking of written work, and of pastoral matters. The agenda for the rest of the training course can be constructed for and by the student from the basis of all of this work.

The above observation example, then, is useful in pointing up many of the issues which must be faced at some point when observation in school is considered. Not only does it indicate the kind of scrutiny to which schools are opening themselves in collaborating in this kind of work, but it also raises issues about observation itself, indicates the vital need for proper partnership between tutor, teacher, and student, and shows the many levels at which one can investigate and be investigated. It raises issues, for example, about the experience needed to *interpret* what has been seen, and about the lack of context which a visitor to a school often experiences when trying to understand what they are seeing. It raises the question about the student's ability to observe closely at all, let alone her ability to sort out the major from the minor details, the significant from the less significant. Implicit in the process of observation and reflection as well as in that which is observed is its value-based nature. Students (and sometimes teachers) take time to unravel this, and need help in doing so. One useful approach here is a deliberate focusing on those crucial distinctions, omnipresent in educational activity, between what people think they are doing, what they say they are doing, what they appear to others to be doing, and what in fact they are doing.

Day visits

By contrast to the above fictional observation sheet (Figure 1), the following documents have been used within a larger programme of school-based work. Figure 2 (on p.110) was designed for use by a group of 16 students on the second of five day visits in the first part of a PGCE secondary course; Figure 3 (on p.111) was designed for use by a group of 15 students on a first visit during the fifth week of a BEd primary course. Figure 2 shows the questions for use in a number of lessons in different subjects, on the same day in the same school, observed by various members of a group of 16 students who were training to teach six different subjects. They had already also talked about these issues in college before the visit and read about them immediately after it. It should be emphasised that these schedules had been carefully negotiated with all relevant school staff who will have seen them and had the opportunity to comment on them.

Perhaps the most important characteristics of these observation schedules are:

> **What Sort of Activity is Teaching?**
>
> Watch the lesson. Try to deduce its plan, shape, rhythm. Write on this paper. Do not show this sheet to pupils.
>
> 1. What are the lesson's intentions/objectives?
>
>   (How do you know/How do pupils know?)
>
> 2. What special resources or materials are used?
>
>   (What special preparation was done beforehand?)
>
> 3. How were pupils organised physically and mentally?
>
> 4. Exactly how was the lesson introduced?
>
> 5. What were the key stages of the lesson?
>   Time   key activities   key instructions   key questions
>
> 6. How were the different working speeds catered for?
>
> 7. How was the lesson drawn to a conclusion?
>
> 8. What were the clearing up instructions?
>
> 9. What do you think were the main deviations from the teacher's plan?
>
>   (Ask if you are right.)
>
> 10. How do you think the teacher would describe his/her role in relation to the learning here?
>
>   (What signals tell you this?)

Figure 2: What sort of activity is teaching?

- The focus in each case, though narrow, is not skills-based.
- The intentions of the schedule were discussed beforehand with school staff and students, and everyone was familiar with them.
- The content had been freshly negotiated from a previous year's schedule to suit
    (a) the context in which they were used
    (b) to take account of the other pressures and demands on both the teachers and the students in the lesson
    (c) to fit a very specific programme designed to prepare students for

Pupils and Learning

Work with the pupils as staff require. Try, at least at some points, to observe the whole class. Use the questions below to help you think, to help you see what to look for. Don't look for every category, focus in where you can. Where you are in a group, work together to cover different aspects among you. These are only GUIDELINES.

1. How is the children's learning organised?

   How is the room organised?

   On what basis have pupils been grouped?

2. What are they intended to learn during this session?

3. How are their differences catered for?

4. Look at two children in detail:
   What are they learning?

   How are they learning it?

   What successes are they having?

   What problems – if any?

5. What motivates this class to work?

Figure 3: Pupils and Learning

   their first teaching practice by addressing some of the basic classroom issues and some of the basic classroom skills.
- The teachers involved knew about and understood the overall programme into which this work fitted.
- The questions required the students to use a range of observational techniques, and to exercise judgement as they recorded information (this issue is raised in the debriefing).
- The students had begun to understand the subjectivity involved, and already appreciated that there was more to observation than they had yet experienced.
- These schedules provided the basic agenda for the reflection sessions which were planned to follow, on teaching and learning in the lessons observed, and on observation itself.

Student perspectives

The following is an attempt to provide some examples of actual reactions to and reflections upon the kind of practice described above. All of the comments were made during or at the end of the first six weeks of a PGCE secondary course. This period contained five one-day visits to a comprehensive school, and the entire programme was planned as an introduction to the first teaching practice, immediately following. The debriefing sessions consisted wherever possible of teacher(s) as well as tutor. The comments are drawn from 11 of the 16 students in the group. Reflection involved debriefing seminar sessions on the school site as well as later in college, but in addition students were required to keep a diary in which they recorded the whole range of their responses (affective and cognitive) to the visits and the immediate debriefing. They were also required to read and share a range of related articles, after the school-based debriefing and before the college-based one. Their oral and written comments show an encouraging range of developing insights.

First reactions

The general reaction manifested early on to the observation and reflection sessions, compared with their pre-course experience, is summed up by JG in an oral comment:

> I valued most the chance to get in and see the lessons and the chance to talk about them afterwards. Otherwise it becomes a habit to go into a lesson and just sit there. If you don't know what you are looking for you don't see much. Here we did. (JG)

Some critical insights

But lest it should seem that students are not drawn by this work to think critically about what they see, it is important to consider the following comments. These include one from DW, after watching a third-year drama group:

> Mrs P exhibited all the 'broken rules' of an experienced teacher in the way she handled them. She worked on a very friendly, almost motherly basis. She actually called one of them darling!
>
> It was interesting to see that when pupils were given more responsibility in relation to their learning, they showed a greater interest in it. (DW)

This is a priniciple often not recognised until late in the first teaching practice.

The following two comments came from students who observed the same second-year science lesson:

> Is the idea of teaching slow learners in ordinary classrooms working? Two boys on one table were alone and distinct – physically separate from the rest of the group – with the second teacher. (JG)

> What was interesting was that a remedial teacher sat in with two of the class helping them during the lesson. At one point during a question and answer session

she told the pupil the answer. This gave the pupil more confidence when he answered in front of the class. In fact, I think, the whole purpose of having a remedial teacher in any class is to give the slower pupils more confidence, rather than just to help them learn and understand. (JW)

The wealth of material for further discussion in these two different reactions is obvious. And such discussion begins where the student 'starts'.

Particularly interesting are the comments of NB. He wrote about a first-year history lesson in which the aim of the lesson, which was held in the library, was to teach certain reference skills.

> Once again this type of activity was new to me. These are skills you pick up in time anyway, but to introduce them at the beginning of a course was an inspired move.
>
> The most able pupils were not necessarily the first to complete the forms. Most pupils seemed motivated because the work was interesting.
>
> Once again, there was very little telling in this lesson. Learning here is the pupils being given signposts to follow, but making their own way – not led to a destination required by the teacher. (NB)

Here eyes are being opened both to a whole new way of working, and to new items on the agenda for learning. The same student was, however, initially at least, somewhat less enthusiastic about a third-year history lesson, based on Schools Council materials.

> The pupils are presented with the facts of an historical event (here the Marie Celeste) and given several theories about it. By intelligent discussion they are to express their opinions on the theories . . . and make up their own minds.
>
> My only reservation about this approach is that you don't get much detail about the event itself – none of the little details that bring history to life (ie, the careers of the sailors to date, where the ship had been). Since so much time is spent on the pupils' discussions, the facts themselves are not as numerous as I personally would enjoy. I can't help thinking that pupils will end up with a very over-superficial view of history, which all the discussion in the world won't help.
>
> Here, then, was a lesson split 50/50 between process and product. Facts of the case were limited (product), but their discussion and investigation (process) was very thorough. I'd perhaps personally prefer more product here (perhaps a 75/25 per cent split) but can see the arguments for both. (NB)

What is particularly pleasing about this extract is the careful delineation of what has been seen and the reactions to it, including the gradual grasping of a new vision of what it was about. Equally pleasing is the sense that the student feels free to find his own preferred balance, while acknowledging both sides. There can be little doubt in this case that being made to write about his experiences forced him to articulate and recognise them, and provided the basis from which to extend his thinking further.

Some sharp words

But there is another range of reactions to this work, some of which gave pause for thought to the participating teachers. Again, these comments show a properly critical approach on the part of the student, and although some comments merely reveal their lack of practical experience, they do also show how sharply prospective teachers will focus upon professional issues.

For example, WB noted thoughtfully that:

> Some teachers are vastly more conscious of what they are doing and how they prepared for it than I expected. (WB)

But there were other experiences too. For example:

> It took ten minutes for the books to be handed out . . . . They were not using their own initiative (maybe they couldn't). . . . The teacher said that they had had discussions before, but that the groups didn't know what to do. (JB watching fifth-year community studies class)

> I did feel that the whole lesson was extremely rushed, although none of the class seemed to complain. (JS of a third-year history lesson taken by the deputy head)

> Pupils were given conflicting instructions. The teacher explained (to us) that the lesson wasn't really prepared because he was a union representative and so carrying out a lot of duties at home (JG of a third-year history lesson)

> Constant noise and walking around – very difficult for those who really want to work to do so. Teacher talks over the din. For ME the ground rules would have to be tighter. I would have become very ratty. (JD on a first-year English lesson)

> The lesson this week was very structured. Manesh, who in previous weeks had disrupted the class, was quiet and got on with his work, something that the other less able pupils also seemed to do. The cost of this was that the more able got bored and talked among themselves. (RP on a third-year RE lesson)

> After the lesson the teacher informed me that she had actually deviated quite considerably from her own lesson plan to accommodate a severely disturbed pupil . . . . The fact that the teaching method could be so dictated seemed to me to be a matter for concern, especially as what the teacher was going to do with them was definitely more exciting.
> This left me with a number of reservations about the benefit of mixed ability classes . . . . However, I did learn how important it is that the teacher is able to adapt and be flexible. (AI on the same RE lesson)

> The class teacher was late because of problems with one child in her family. There was a disagreement between her and some of the pupils about what she had asked them to do for homework. There is obviously a need to know exactly what you have set. She then had to leave the class to get equipment because she had been late and had not had a chance to collect it beforehand. (JG on a third-year science lesson)

> The class of 16 assembled on the field to commence work. The deputy headteacher's aims were to show the principles of heading. Afterwards he came up and said 'There you are, it's a doddle, isn't it?' But he didn't teach them anything! (JC of a third-year PE lesson)

Debriefing based upon these reactions is clearly able to take up almost all the issues of a training agenda. Particularly, they provide excellent material for consideration of the values brought up to the observation and interpretation of practice.

Reflections upon observation

The place of reflection and deliberation

Fostering learning through such practice involves having a range of ways of reflecting (for example, oral discussion and written diary), and several separate occasions upon which the debriefing from the practice takes place. These need to include an occasion as soon after the practical observation as possible – preferably immediately afterwards. Here the students (who will have seen five or six lessons between them), together with the tutor (who will have flitted between those lessons), and as many of the teachers as possible, can work together. There also needs to be an occasion, about a day later, for further reflection, after reading and thinking have taken place. It is possible to plan these separate sessions so that the initial reflections are more concerned with the instrumental aspects of the lesson, and later sessions are focused on deliberation about the wider educational issues.

Consideration of the observation techniques themselves is also important, and can be illustrated by drawing on the range of perspectives available on the lesson. For this reason it is helpful for two or three students to work in one classroom together, and for about 16 to be assigned to one school.

The role of the teacher and the tutor

The role of the teacher and tutor is vital in both the observed session and the debriefing. The teacher provides the main focus during the practical work, but the tutor needs to be involved in the classroom too.

The procedures used by the teacher (and tutor) during the observation session, and by tutor (and teacher) during the debriefing, need to have been talked through by both, including exploring together what each can best bring to the observation and the debriefing session. This does *not*, however, involve entirely programming either event beforehand. This would fail to capitalise on the very aspect of real practice which is both important and is unable to be reproduced in any other conditions – namely its unpredictable and essentially messy nature. They will need to improvise. Since this is the very nature of the work which students themselves will be doing in classrooms as teachers, it is fitting that this is how teacher and tutor operate, and that they ultimately discuss this with the students.

The place of observation in the course as a whole

There are really three uses of observation during the initial training course. They are:

  – to enable the student to begin to come to grips with the issues and the

activities of being a teacher
- to enable the student to begin to see the complexities of real practical situations
- to enable the student to refine her own thinking about how she will wish to proceed during practical work herself.

To suit these three main purposes, there are three main occasions on which observation of practice is a major aspect of the training. These are:

A   Pre-course experience. Observation is used here in order to begin to initiate the student into the ways of thinking about teaching, learning, education and schooling, as a teacher rather than a pupil.

B   Intermittent experience. This usually means experience of observation before the first teaching practice. Here, observation together with reflection and deliberation tend to be aimed at opening up the complexity of practical issues, and to encouraging the student to begin to consider her own preferred mode of operation.

C   Pre-practice experience. This is used at various stages in the course when the student is beginning to be acclimatised to the school in which she will do her own teaching practice.

The practical implications

For teachers

This technique makes very considerable demands on teachers in respect of time and effort. In the present climate of Directed Time this will need to be acknowledged by schools and LEAs. Since it clearly involves staff development it ought to rate GRIST funding, and government recognition. Teachers involved will experience the following needs:

- to be prepared to be observed, to be able to think aloud on their feet afterwards, and to respond positively to the students' reactions
- to be familiar with observation techniques
- to have spent considerable time in planning the practical work and establishing a working understanding with the tutor
- to ensure the compatibility of the students' needs and those of their own pupils
- to work with their own colleagues within the school to extend the understandings of these training methods, since all staff will be involved at least indirectly.

For all these outgoings teachers will gain in terms of having been part of an enterprise in which everyone learns together and where what they learn will have a direct bearing upon their own work in class.

For tutors

For tutors the demands are also considerable. They include all of those listed for teachers. Most particularly they involve demands upon planning time. The planning for this work, much of which will occur at the very beginning of the training course, needs to have been set up well before the beginning of the academic year. This will mean working with senior staff and a range of teachers, in the previous summer, so that all those taking part know and understand what is involved. It will also mean knowing the school from the inside. It is helpful, just prior to the students' visits, to have taught the class in which observation will occur, and to know the workings of others. The tutor will need to prepare students to respond to observations professionally but critically, and will need to be able to cope with any ethical issues which arise from this. These are part of the necessary risks of learning, and are a legitimate part of students' learning. Like the teacher, the tutor will gain enormously in terms of insights into teaching and learning as a result of this work.

For students

The most important implications of this work for students are that they will find themselves working hard on day visits and will need to give time and energy to logging them during and afterwards. They will also need to be prepared to think on their feet during the observation and the debriefing. The advantages of these demands are that they all relate directly to the skills, abilities, and capacities that will be needed in the teaching profession.

Arguably, the advantages outweigh the demands for all those involved.

8. Cooperative Teaching and Cooperative Learning: Team Teaching as a Training Technique

Summary

- Team teaching: the theory
  — its past and future
  — its chief characteristics
  — its potential in teacher education
  — its place in initial training
- Team teaching without the teacher
  — the context
  — the aims
  — the main stages
  — the roles of teacher and tutor
- Perspectives on practice
  — student comment
  — data from questionnaire
- Reflections on the technique
  — organisation
  — the intentions
  — the tutor's responsibilities
  — the teacher's role
- Some implications for practice
  — three practical preconditions

Introduction

This chapter attempts to present a version of teaching which students in initial training can use to extend their practical experience and explore their own perspectives on both practice and themselves. Unusually, this approach is best attempted without the presence in the classroom of either the teacher or the tutor. But this certainly does not mean that teacher and tutor have no role in the entire proceedings.

Team teaching: the theory

Its past and future

Although Hatton has recently said that the heyday of team teaching was in the 1960s and 1970s (Hatton, 1985, p. 228), it is neither dead nor is it likely to die.

Not only is it still alive in the primary sector of British education, but it is due for a long life there because of the sheer influence of the number of open-plan schools built in the 1960s. Further, it is now, in the late 1980s, spreading fairly extensively to the secondary sector under a number of contemporary influences. Briefly, these are:

1. The increasing attempt to bridge the transition gap between primary and secondary by using a number of primary school approaches in the early years of the secondary school.
2. The increased pressure on teaching resources brought about by the integration of subjects in the secondary school (though this may be modified with the National Curriculum).
3. An increasing emphasis on cooperative work at both pupil and teacher level in secondary school.
4. The pressures and problems of discipline in some schools, which mean that teachers are beginning to prefer to work together.
5. The Education Act 1981 (implemented 1983) has required the remedial or special needs staff to leave their own departmental areas and to be present in ordinary classes to help the special needs pupils within them.
6. The influences of the 'new' teaching styles and methods brought in to secondary schools via: Technical and Vocational Education (TVE)– which has as one of its key objectives staff collaboration between and within institutions; the General Certificate of Secondary Education (GCSE); and the Certificate of Pre-Vocational Education (CPVE).
7. The new approaches to teacher appraisal and self-evaluation call for teachers working more closely together at the level of planning and evaluation.

In addition to all of these influences, as a result of the current pressure of egalitarian ideals, there are also societal trends towards partnership, collaboration and teamwork, and against competition and individuality.

These trends clearly show that experience of team teaching will be of direct use to both the primary and secondary student. So, what are the main characteristics of this kind of work, and how do they compare with the more traditional individual teaching methods?

Its chief characteristics

In Hatton's words, team teaching 'requires shared responsibility by two or more teachers for all pupils at the level of planning, implementation and evaluation' (Hatton, 1985, p.229). This means that team teaching requires teachers to work together at the planning stage, discussing and negotiating the curriculum, including the aims, intentions, the content, and the teaching and learning methods. It also involves teaching in front of each other in the classroom, thus opening up all the teacher activity to critical scrutiny by the team as a whole, and it means meeting afterwards to discuss what has happened and to plan, or replan, the next work.

As Hatton explains, this challenges a number of fundamental tenets held by teachers which have arisen from their work in more traditional and closed classrooms. These include the teachers' traditional valuing of privacy, autonomy, and individualised practices (Hatton, 1985, p.232). Thus, teachers lose the privacy of their classroom and have aural and visual contact with each other, have to find an agreed way of working which takes account of the ideology of the rest of the team, and in some cases have to give up some of their more individualistic methods and even relationships with pupil groups.

Its potential in teacher education

These very characteristics of team teaching mean that it has the potential to revolutionise the way teachers view their own work. It can open up, to challenge and to exploration, ideas teachers hold about teaching, learning, classroom management, themselves, their pupils, and the curriculum. This is simply because once all work is carried out as a team at the planning, execution, and evaluation stages, then discussion, explanation, and analysis become unavoidable and are bound under normal circumstances to lead to professional growth. Further, as the team grows in experience, it usually grows in the enjoyment of sharing.

There are, of course, potential problems also. For example, in serving teachers who have been long accustomed to working alone in their classrooms there will be initial fears and awkwardness to overcome, and the need for greater explanations and negotiation to come to terms with. Providing this stage is not solved by ducking back out into another form of (non) team teaching by dividing the work up and reverting exclusively to individualistic approaches, however, these very problems can be the beginning of new thinking. For example, they often reveal that the individual's fears, problems, and unsolved worries are in fact held in common. This in itself can provide the basis of a new willingness to share ideas. With the advent of self-evaluation, these approaches are likely to become more rather than less significant.

Persuading long-serving teachers who have worked for many years on their own to take up these methods can be difficult. Certainly, placing staff in a team and expecting this to work without problem is sheer folly, though encouraging staff to find someone to team up with whose work does not threaten them can be successful.

But of course, these issues do not arise if the teachers involved are still in training. To some extent, therefore (indeed, to a greater extent than it used to be), it is important to offer all students experience of team teaching during their initial training. And this is the case *despite* the government survey conducted as part of *The New Teacher in School* (DES, 1982), in which students declared that their training experiences of team teaching were of little use to them. After all, those comments were not only highly subjective but were pronounced within two terms of the first year of their careers. Further, that survey was undertaken near the beginning of the 1980s, when many of the reasons for the re-emergence of team teaching cited above were only just arising.†

What, then, are the real possibilities for team teaching in initial training?

Its place in initial training

Team teaching during teaching practice has been a problem from the point of view of sustained school experience. Here, after all, the student is expected to show what she can achieve on her own, without an experienced teacher helping her. Further, the *supervision* of a student in a team-teaching situation can be a diplomatic nightmare, for reasons that hardly need elaborating upon.

Even quite recently in a number of London comprehensives I have found difficulty in getting staff to see the need (on a final practice) for a balance of lessons which allows for a real range of the student's own solo work to be displayed to internal and external examiners as well as seen by the supervisor. This is partly a result of the overprotective attitude that many staff still have to students, and is also a result of the fact that more and more secondary lessons are run on a team basis. There is a distinction between lessons in which special needs support staff are present (where the student is fully responsible for the direction of the lesson, including liaising beforehand with the special needs teacher), and the full team-teaching situation, where, still, the weaker student is (unhelpfully) covered by the lead-taking, experienced teacher.

The technique described below, however, offers students a new classroom experience in which *neither* the teacher nor the tutor are present in the classroom. Here, during intermittent school experience, two or three students can work together in one classroom and gain the normal advantages of team teaching plus some understanding of what it entails in terms of negotiation.

Team teaching without the teacher

The following practical example and associated theoretical perspectives are drawn from West London's secondary PGCE course in 1986, but the basic work could just as usefully be applied to PGCE primary, or to BEd secondary or primary courses.

The context

The most important aspects of the context of this work are that it takes place *after* the first teaching practice (in the case of the example below, in the second

---

† See page 197.

term of the secondary PGCE course). Here students were placed back in their original intermittent school experience school, which they again visited for one entire day per week. During this day, and across five weeks, they worked in small teams of two or three students, each team teaching one class for one 70-minute session per week. The work followed closely the syllabus which the class teacher had already planned. To this extent the students had to put into operation work which was not of their own choosing, though they had the choice about the methods, as long as the class teacher agreed them. In practice, this lack of choice over content was actually helpful at this point.

The aims

The aims and intentions of this work are quite complex, and derive mainly from the characteristics of team teaching listed above, and from the position in the course of this work (that is, that it follows the first practice and is in no sense assessed or even supervised in the classroom itself). There are five main intentions, some of which are interrelated.

The first is to help the student learn more about herself (in terms of beliefs, abilities, values, strengths, weaknesses, attitudes, skills). This is important at the stage where some habits, skills, and capacities are beginning to be formed (as a result of the first practice), but when they are far from being hardened into one inflexible way of working. After the first practice, when the student has gained some confidence and begun to learn some of the techniques that she finds personally comfortable, team teaching is a good means of persuading the student to look afresh at her own ways of working and to think critically about these in comparison with the preferences of fellow team members. At this point students are also well motivated to challenge each other and to sharpen their own thinking in response to the challenges of their fellows. To this extent the experience is one which is investigative. Students use the opportunity to investigate their own and each others' methods.

In addition to learning more about themselves, students continue, via this technique, to learn about classroom management, pupils' abilities and learning capabilities, and teaching strategies. Again, these become matters of dispute and temporary resolution as students find that different personalities in teachers and pupils lead to variable results even from the same techniques. This very properly opens up to their real experience the problematic and value-based nature of the teacher's work in education. This in turn is calculated to open the student to a more flexible approach to educational decision-making, and to being prepared to continue to learn beyond the initial training stage.

Students also investigate the whole procedure of team teaching itself, uncovering through their own experience (and their reading) the essential differences between this way of operating in the classroom, and the more traditional ways of doing so. By this means they not only discover the theoretical differences in operating singly and in a team, but also begin to come to terms with what working cooperatively means to them personally. This enables students to begin to think about their own preferred modes of operation, and in addition, alerts them to the implications which underlie the team-teaching situation.

Fourth, this work enables students, as part of their formal assessment, to investigate and write about an issue related to their main and subsidiary subjects, and to contribute further practical experience to the college-based method seminars.

Closely allied to this is the final intention, which is to offer the student a wider experience of practical teaching in a school other than her teaching practice school, and an arena for exploring teaching methods which is 'safe' from formal TP assessment.

If these are the intentions, then, how is the activity operated?

The main stages

Briefly, there are six stages which are vital to the proper operation of this particular version of team teaching. Some of these are additional to the normal organising of team teaching, and are the result of the teacher and the tutor both being absent from the main classroom action.

The key stages then are as follows.

1. The observation stage
For the first week the student team sit in with the class and their normal teacher, allowing for a smooth take-over in the following week and discussions with the class teacher about the work. This stage is necessary for the student team to sum up the pupils, methods, levels of work, and the normal working traditions of the class. It also provides students with an opportunity to put into professional practice the observation techniques which were learnt and used on intermittent school experience in their first term. The importance of keen observation in the classroom becomes very clear.

2. The negotiative stage
This needs to take place at two levels in order that there is smooth transition between the normal class teacher and the 'new' team. Thus, there need to be two kinds of negotiation: negotiation with the original teacher (about the lesson content, methods, and resources); and then negotiation within the team (about how the work will be planned, executed, and evaluated). At both levels the student learns much, which cannot be learnt elsewhere on the course, about working with colleagues, planning alongside them, and finding a shared view of the work and how to evaluate it. The planning of what to evaluate and how it can be monitored within the lesson and by whom, automatically becomes a part of this pre-lesson planning. Thus, all roles and strategies need to be carefully considered and agreed.

3. The classroom action stage
The students work in a normal sized class and classroom, and can be sure that they will not normally be interrupted by tutor or teacher and will not be assessed. Within the classroom, the team is encouraged to find a variety of ways of operating across the four weeks available to them. The normal lesson length of 70 minutes also allows for a variety of teaching and learning strategies within the lesson and a change of leader. Students whose first week of planning was not detailed enough quickly learn that team teaching makes more rather than less demands on staff. Most teams quickly discover the need to assign broad responsibilities, but also to make on-the-spot decisions which take account of their fellow team members.

They learn to watch each other more carefully, and gradually begin to lay bare their own theories and the unplanned variables which a teacher must cope with. And with the introduction of other teachers a whole new range of variables comes into play. They are also brought up against some of their own individual strengths and weaknesses, but at least they see others facing the same experience. (Again, this is often not true on teaching practice, which can leave a student much more isolated.) Perhaps surprisingly, there is considerably less attempt by pupils than might have been expected to play one student off against another, and on the whole pupils benefit from a far greater range of individual attention.

4. The evaluation stage
This stage is handled at three levels. First, students are encouraged to debrief each other in terms of each other's performance in class and in terms of what each observed and was aware of across all of the characteristics of the lesson. Some teams will choose to concentrate on different things in each week, and some will allow the observer to decide what will be observed, while some require the person observed to dictate the terms. In addition to this, the issue of team teaching itself if also an agenda item. Second, teams report to and are debriefed by the teacher. Finally, there is a group debriefing, led by the tutor, where teams share what they have learnt week by week.

5. The log write-up
The school experience log, which is part of the assessment procedure, is used to record the planning, the group and the individual lesson appraisal, and any useful additional items which arose from the group debriefing, and the teachers' debriefing.

6. The appraisal of team teaching itself
At the end of the whole five weeks, the issues of team teaching itself are discussed at length by the entire group of students, the teachers, and the tutor.

The roles of teacher and tutor

The role of the teacher is quite a complex one despite the fact (or because of the fact) that he is not involved in the team itself. He must be prepared to be observed with his class during the first week, and to spend as much preparation time as is necessary to provide the student team with all that they need to take over the class. This can become more difficult when the teacher sees the class in an intervening lesson before the following week. The teacher debriefs the team, often about the pupils' work and reactions. He is also invited to attend whole-group debriefing sessions.

The tutor has to set up the entire operation. He must also establish the atmosphere in which errors, failures, and problems are tackled positively at all times. This is part of his task during all of the debriefing periods.

Perspectives on practice

It has only proved possible to record the reactions to this technique of the 16 students involved in this work in one secondary school, even though the scheme lasted over three years and involved four schools per year. Their views on the processes set up were sought by means of two questionnaries. The first of these was on team teaching itself; the second was the normal course evaluation questionnaire given to students at the end of their taught course. In addition, it has also been possible to draw upon the written comments in students' diary-logs (required as part of their assessment work), as well as via their oral contributions privately and in seminar. The views of the teachers involved have only been expressed informally in ordinary conversation, partly because the Teachers' Action has precluded detailed additional discussion and involvement in debriefings. The views of pupils have not been investigated systematically, although they do come through some of the students' evaluations. My views as tutor can be deduced from the rest of this chapter.

Student comment

The general questionnaire responses showed almost universal praise for the opportunity to teach in an unpressured way in a second school environment and without the oversight of a supervisor. The most succinct version of this stated:

> Returning to an environment where one had initially experienced some insecurity and trauma reinforced and consolidated the changes in attitude and increase in confidence that have since been made.

Apart from this, the key comments about team teaching mainly declared it to have been a demanding (but useful) experience, which allowed students to see how other people used different methods and different emphases.

While students were in the process of preparing and negotiating their team teaching there was much anxiety about this process. At this point (for many it was for the first time), the group became aware that we all operate on the basis of our own individual views and values, and that negotiating across these is not always easy. They had little choice in whom they worked with since the subject was the deciding factor. This did mean that they often had to work with people who had very different views. So for most students, the real significance of this stage was that it enabled them to experience the real implications of what they had previously only mouthed in the first term, that education is value based. They crystallised the key tensions here as arising from the following differences:

— attitudes towards *how* pupils should learn
— attitudes to the structuring of work
— attitudes to the use and presentation of written work
— expectations about pupils' abilities
— expectations about the length of concentration on one task
— teacher's response to written work
— approaches to classroom management.

While the list is a patchy one in terms of its varying levels of detail, the discoveries that it encapsulates are certainly in a different league from many made on a solo teaching practice, where any differences between student and teacher can be (are usually) put down to differences of age and experience, and thus dismissed. Here, the students had to face the fact that though they were all at the same stage of training, there were deep differences of view which had not emerged while they were merely sparring with each other in the safety of the seminar during their first-term visits.

These differences became crucial in the classroom and particularly at the level of classroom management. Here, however well the team had negotiated and agreed an approach, the unexpected and unplanned incidents brought out instinctive and different responses. These provided the teams with considerable talking points after the lesson, and became the point of departure for the next lot of planning. Such incidents were not seen by anyone as destructive of the lesson or the students, and this was partly because the number of adults per class ensured that there was remarkably little attempt by pupils to make capital out of the differences. These issues also highlighted the differences in approach to classroom management between solo and team teaching.

Data from questionnaire

The main questionnaire on team teaching itself threw up useful comments across a number of categories. Many of these, though not original in essence, show the students' process of learning. The comments reported below indicate that it has taken some students until the second term of their three-term course to begin to assimilate many of the issues raised in the first term and to orient themselves towards thinking educationally. They therefore represent a step forward in the *students'* understanding, and represent for them a real sign of progress, because they are not made in imitation of what someone else has said, but spring from reflection upon their own practical experience.

As might be expected, the key issues which surfaced in the questionnaire were discipline, planning, and team techniques.

Most replies mentioned the greater security in discipline arising from working in a team, though two students raised the negative side of the frustration of not being able to do things their own way. Most felt that they had learnt a lot about planning. Typical comments in reply to the question, 'What have you learnt from negotiating and planning with your team?' were:

— it takes a lot of planning
— working with someone else threw up new angles
— negotiating – friendly or not – helps us focus on our aims and intentions
— it does make you think more about the planning of lessons. Content must be negotiated with others, and your ideas may be rejected
— it can prove rather difficult and requires alot (sic) of compromising on behalf of group members
— all members of a team need to be sold on the idea behind a lesson
— I learnt that three student teachers can have very different ideas and beliefs about ways of teaching.

The question, 'What are the differences between teaching as a team and working on your own?' produced the following two groups of response.

Those who saw the positive sides argued that team teaching provided the following kinds of benefit:

— helps discipline, classroom management, the distribution of resources
— benefits the teacher organisationally and leads to more fluent lessons
— helps if the teacher at the front is stuck for a word
— much more and much better individual attention for all pupils
— much more time for the two extreme ends of the mixed ability range
— pupils benefit because there is more time to monitor groups, invidiuals and to spot good and original work
— you are more open to inspection.

Interestingly, this last comment was firmly placed in the advantages category, the additional shrewd comment being added that 'being observed makes you more observant'.

The following represent the main comments on the other side:

— I feel happier when I am on my own, then I can say what I like
— you can't be as innovative as you would like due to other people's preferences
— thinking on your feet is more difficult because of the need to remember other people in the team
— I feel very self-conscious
— sheer survival in class to some extent got in the way of the debriefing and reflection required.

All of these are of course important starting points for further discussion with students.

There was a considerable range of replies to the questions, 'What did other team members teach you?' All showed a commendable willingness to learn from each other, perhaps rating it as less painful than learning from or with a tutor. What was learnt was similar to what tutors and teachers would have been attempting to teach them. But this learning was under less pressure, and seemed to result in a more genuine acceptance and a better assimilation of it. The kinds of learning reported included:

— to lower my voice
— different approaches
— different levels of tolerance
— a more relaxed approach
— better relationships with pupils
— the need for a more imaginative approach to planning
— to be more adventurous
— the advantage of setting clear, firm standards in task setting, from the start
— that it is important to be able to explain your ideas well enough for all members of the team to understand. If not, how will the pupils?

It is remarkable how much like supervisors' comments most of these voluntary *written* comments sound.

Similar kinds of insight arose from the question, 'What have you learnt from team teaching that you could not have learnt by working alone?' Here responses included the following:

— we all make similar mistakes
— you get a better chance to look at the class and its response to various activities
— that there are different methods that can reach the same end
— that the things that happen in a classroom can be viewed from many different angles
— that the social interaction in a classroom is very complex.

These reactions also show, perhaps indirectly, that pupils are likely to gain more than they might lose from the experience. It is more difficult however, without proper investigation, to be sure how class teachers viewed all of this. Two points have arisen with regularity over the three years of this work, however. They are that much non-teaching time is needed by the class teacher at the planning end and at the debriefing end. This need is the greater because the teacher is not going to appear at all in the classroom.

The second point is that, even where negotiation between tutor and teacher has been very detailed, the teacher is still often doubtful about how much to tell the students, how much to expect of them, and how sharply to draw the constraints. This is bound to be a problem, but to some extent teachers will begin to be more aware of how to play this the more frequently they are involved in it, and *the more time they have to spend planning with the tutor beforehand.* I believe that the kinds of things that students can gain from this experience (as evidenced above) considerably outweigh these problems, and make it worth working on improving the technique and its structuring.

Reflections on the technique

Like all problem-solving approaches to learning, the success of team-teaching activity depends largely upon how well it is prepared for and how well it is supported. Many of the following comments therefore will concentrate on those aspects.

Organisation

Although the above student comments naturally demonstrate that this way of teaching is more congenial to some people than to others, there were no suggestions at any point in the proceedings that the activity itself was regarded as not worth attempting. Rather, their comments were on the need for tighter structuring. These comments included the need to 'push harder' the reflective aspects, the need to structure more carefully the kinds of evaluation required, and the need to require as an absolute that the team's joint scheme and a joint evaluation be required as part of the final written work. These comments represent helpful ways forward to improving the working of the scheme.

Perhaps the most worrying result of this particular practice was the team which, in spite of all that was said, still managed to duck out of the team approach, and divide up their class so that each simply taught a group. This does seem to indicate that there was a need for greater control, so that at least they all had the basic experience of team teaching, even if they preferred other ways of operating.

The intentions

This brings us to crucial points about the use of this particular technique. It is not an attempt to convert the teaching profession to team teaching, and it is important that the students understand this. It is simply an experience that offers students:

— a secure opportunity to discover more about themselves
— experience of the range of views likely to be held by colleagues
— the experience of negotiating with equal colleagues across these views
— the chance to learn a little more about the classroom and the pupils in it because there is slightly less need to take full responsibility for the progress of learning all of the time
— the chance to become slightly detached and to observe more calmly as a result.

The tutor's responsibilities

The tutor's responsibilities are clearly considerable in negotiating and setting up the work and in providing a wide variety of opportunities for debriefing and reflection. Like all methods of this kind, the quality of commitment by the tutor and teacher to the technique will largely determine the amount of benefit gained by the students. Both teacher and tutor need to have carried out much the same process of negotiation which the students follow, and, of course, the tutor must do this with every teacher involved.

The teacher's role

The teacher's role, as has been implied, also requires considerable time, a certain willingness to be observed and to discuss this work afterwards, a willingness to give up a class for one period per week across one complete month, and an ability to play the work by ear to some extent, week by week, as the students' team work progresses. Like many of these situations, one of the hardest things for the teacher is to avoid doing (or redoing) the students' work.

Some implications for practice

Like most innovations, the greatest problem in the early stages is the failure at *both* school and college level to allow additional time to teachers and tutors while the preliminary stages are planned and negotiated. Like all that was done in education before Directed Time, this work was carried out on the backs of those who were willing to give up their own time to 'get it right'. It is very unlikely, following government intervention over teachers' pay and conditions (DES, 1987), that staff will ever again be willing to take on these duties in their own time. The following, therefore, is a list of practical preconditions without which this kind of work will not flourish in future.

Three practical preconditions

1. School staff need to be properly and officially timetabled to prepare and monitor this work. They need time to see the tutor, the student team, and to be involved in the range of debriefings as well as to look at the written work that the students produce *both* in preparation for their teaching *and* as a result of their teaching. This latter includes reading the diary-logs. But seeing the returns of questionnaires is also important, and this means spending time with the tutor perhaps after the end of the whole programme. If this were done, it would of course constitute a major and valuable programme of staff development *for everyone* involved. It is sometimes suggested to me when I raise these issues in school that it is impossible to plan a year's timetable to accommodate the work of one half term. I find it hard to believe that were staff, including senior staff, committed to this work, arrangements could not be made. Alternatively, the onus might well be placed upon the college to find ways of facilitating the release of staff.

2. The same is true at the college end. Now that we have become a numbers-game industry, student numbers are being pushed up to keep up the staff/student ratio, and there is less room and less sympathy for more imaginative work. If initial training is a serious enterprise, it should not mean that those who are still enthusiasts for this work must find their own time for the negotiation, debriefing and reflection with school staff.

3. The key implication for the students is that this work, like all problem-solving approaches, takes up considerable time, and is not easily compatible with writing formal essay assignments which can still be required in other parts of the course. This is a matter for course designers.

Generally, this kind of work is threatened by the present demand for quantifiable efficiency and the drag of traditional methods. The only way to fight this is to demonstrate that this kind of opportunity for real learning is worth the time and effort. It is to this end that this chapter is dedicated.

9. School and College Collaboration: Some Successes and Failures

Summary

- The preparation for practice
  — the assumptions of the planning
  — the preparation of the students
  — the school preparations
- The main action
  — the basic plan
  — the first visit
  — subsequent visits
  — the last visit
- Some perspectives on the project
  — from the students
  — from the pupils
  — from the TP student
- Some reflections
  — next time
  — the role of the school staff
  — other possible adaptations

Introduction

An example of a project which experienced mixed success and failure is offered for scrutiny here in the belief that it can provide insight into collaboration between college and school.

The project itself took place for one half day per week across two terms. The students involved were 14 BEd (secondary) students in the second year of their course, who had just returned from their first block of sustained school experience. They were studying English as a subsidiary subject, and the entry qualification for this part of the course was A level English. The school involved was the school where, as a tutor seeking 'recent and relevant experience', I had joined the staff for a one-term exchange with the deputy head.

The pupils chosen for the project were (by request) 26 very disaffected fourth years. The subject, which was planned to operate in school across seven weeks, was English via media studies. The ultimate aim, for *each* of five groups of pupils, was to produce a 15-minute video which presented a portrait of their (school) community as *they* saw it. They were to plan, film, and present the work. Five very sophisticated video cameras from the Institute were made available for this purpose. The students were to be the facilitators of the work, not the executors. It was made clear to the students from the start that this was not a teaching practice, and demanded different skills. It was *not* intended to be a demonstration of what one teacher could achieve with a class. It was a practical workshop in which everyone had something to learn, and of a kind which would not normally be able to happen in a school, except where an institute and a school worked closely together.

The preparation for practice

The assumptions of the planning

The assumptions on which the planning of the work was based fell into three main categories, two of which proved well founded, but one of which proved to be ill-founded.

The first set of assumptions was about the value of action, reflection, and deliberation (as already outlined in earlier chapters). These shaped the timing of the two terms' work, and basically proved to be sound assumptions, even where (or perhaps especially where) there were unexpected snags or failures of execution. A second level of assumptions related to the learning experiences for both pupils and students. Here, it was assumed that work which was essentially school-focused, and ultimately also school-based, was bound to be both motivating and profitable for both the pupils and the students even if it was not totally successful in all respects. These assumptions also proved correct, even though some aspects of what was planned and what was implemented turned out to be overambitious because of the time available.

But those assumptions relating to the school-college relationship and the inevitable value of the project as a partnership experience proved unfounded. It is in order to unravel this complex situation that the following two sections are presented.

The preparation of the students

There were a number of respects in which the students had to be prepared for this work. They needed help in:

— the relatively new techniques of using video cameras
— making coherent film which drew on visual techniques to tell a story or make a documentary comment
— drawing on their knowledge (practical and theoretical) of English literature and language teaching for the new purpose of working in media studies
— learning some of the language and concepts of media studies
— working as a team to prepare and present lessons to a group of pupils

— getting to know the pupils and their work before taking over the group
— drawing on all of this knowledge in order to facilitate the practical work of *others*
— exploiting this work for a range of educational purposes.

The kinds of preparation necessary in the 30 hours available fell roughly into four main concerns. The first concern was to develop quickly a grasp of a range of English teaching issues, including a sharpened awareness of the opportunities for oral work and problem-solving inherent in the planning and filming, and differences between written work and camera work as a means of telling a story or making a comment.

The second concern was to give the students plenty of practical work with cameras, and in this respect the technical assistance available from one member of the Institute's media staff was invaluable. This enabled students to become familiar with the equipment and to try their own hands at making a portrait of their college environment. It also served to point up further the oral work and social skills which this practical work fostered even within their own work.

The school-based work became much easier when it became clear that the chief technician who had helped us was interested enough to come into school for most of the lessons.

The third area of concern was to provide the chance to meet and assess the pupils with whom the practical work would be carried out. This was planned as a visit to one lesson only, but as a result of that visit was immediately extended to a second because of a failure to structure the first meeting satisfactorily, so that students had a real role to play. This failure was increased by the students' difficulty (as a result of having just completed a first teaching practice) in adapting to being teachers in the same classroom together.

These two memorable lessons, in which the room layout played a crucial role, were a very useful base for the students' work, and were discussed in detail afterwards with teacher and tutor. These debriefings were given additional impetus by the fact that the teacher and the tutor had each separately produced an observation list for the work.

Discussion of both these visits, in school and later in college, ranged across the difficulties of 'assessing' pupils on the spot in class, through the content of media studies classes, to the significance of the organisation of the room. These issues left students with plenty to reflect upon ready for their own lesson preparation.

The fourth concern was to allow enough time and assistance for planning the second term's practical work. Six hours of the course were put aside at the end of the first term for this, and here a surprise awaited. The quality of the deliberation which went into the planning of schemes of work and lessons by each student group was extremely high. Students came to grips with educational planning issues of all kinds which they had earlier struggled with both in early college-based work, and during their first teaching practice. Indeed, their thinking and their debates rapidly became as sophisticated as that of final-year students. They benefited from the fact that the planning was 'for real', and had an immediacy about it, yet could gain from the strength of team thinking. They had to get the team work right since I had declared an absolute refusal to step in to cover any problems. Further, the students benefited from the fact that it was not a teaching practice and they were not going to be assessed on their practical teaching, but on their reflections upon how they had fostered the pupils' learning. In order to focus upon this goal the students were encouraged to assess themselves on the evidence of the pupils' learning, creativity, motivation, decision-making, and willingness to try.

Alongside this work also went the preparation of and by the school, and this must be commented upon briefly before turning to the main action.

The school preparations

Since the preparations, both of the school by myself as tutor, and by the school of itself for the students, were the least satisfactory aspect of the whole project they warrant some attention.

The irony of the situation was that *because* I had actually taught in the school, and *because* the head was kind enough to allow me the entire run of the school, and left me to make direct contact with the staff relevant to the project, a number of things went wrong! Because I was regarded as a senior member of staff, and it was assumed that I could set up the work at that level myself, all other contact with senior staff was missing. As a result, all the organisational elements normally carried out by a deputy overseeing such a project were either left undone (since I was not in the school to do them) or were done piecemeal by the staff directly involved in the project. Thus there was too little communication with the rest of the school, and this was a serious omission since pupils (with the students) were filming all over the place.

Further, the preparations for the visits themselves were not tied up beyond the classrooms in which the teaching was to be done. And, most disappointing of all, the staff who were released by the entry of the students, instead of working *with* the project, mostly found priority jobs elsewhere. This was evidence of a lack of expectation that the project and the students' and the pupils' experiences could provide a learning environment for *the school*. It also meant the absence of a very rich dimension in both the debriefing and the further preparation sessions. I was responsible for not having made the point clearly enough that the project was intended to be college and school working together. But, even if this had been more clearly stated, there is evidence that the ever-present pragmatic priorities of the working school would always have taken over. Here we have the 'spare pair of hands notion', which sees the advent of students as freeing the teacher for something else.

The main action

The basic plan

The basic plan for the practical work was for seven visits to school for half a day each in the summer term. The actual lesson was the first hour in the morning, and the second two hours were set aside for debriefing and preparing for the next. The students elected to work with pupils in groups from the beginning and to work towards completion by the end of the sixth session in order that the class could view the work of each group in the final session. For the final session, the school kindly arranged for the pupils to work with us for the first two of the normal three hour-lessons of the morning.

The school requested that the students set and marked homework which related to the video-making, since pupils needed a range of written work for their examination folders. Decisions about what should be set were left to each group, and issues about the place of assessment in experiential learning arose from this. Some pupils and all students kept diaries. Mine was shared with students during debriefing.

The fact that the students worked with pupils in groups, and actually filmed in all kinds of venues across the school, meant that it was never possible for me to see all that happened. But by sheer chance a PGCE student from West London Institute who had an English degree, including film and video, was doing her final TP in the school. She was freed for the first two periods of the day (the teaching hour and the debriefing hour), and took part in the project by observing one group very closely and reporting back on this during the debriefing sessions. Between myself, the technician, and the TP student, therefore, there was a fairly high profile of observation work.

This was, however, one area in which it proved impossible to involve the class teacher, perhaps because he was neither familiar with observation techniques, nor aware of the processes of learning which the project was drawing upon. Whenever he was available, he seemed anxious to talk to me about a range of issues peripheral to the work in hand. There seemed to be no way of overcoming this problem but to avoid sessions with the teacher because they prevented my attention being focused on the students and the pupils. I had too easily assumed that a freed teacher would naturally wish to join in; would understand the learning processes at work for the students; would be able to use a knowledge of how to observe; and would be aware of the importance of this for debriefing. It had been too easy to forget the pressures of a working school and a busy department, and to overlook the fact that the school, though a very experienced TP school, was not used to this sort of work.

The sections which follow attempt to describe two visits in detail (the first and the last), and to pick out major issues only from the intervening ones.

The first visit

On the first session the students had to establish themselves with the pupils, and to explain to the pupils what the project was about. This they chose to do from the beginning in individual groups.

Most groups had planned to use the first session for three kinds of familiarisation procedures. They had taken on board the need for the groups of pupils and students to get to know each other; they had realised the need for pupils to show them round the school and to look at the school in order to decide how to present it on film; and they had foreseen the need to establish familiarity and safety routines with cameras.

Although there were other areas of the school available to them, four out of five groups of students elected to start work in the 'base' hut where I observed them. Thus, the PGCE TP student (hereafter referred to as TP) was asked to observe the one group which elected to work away from the rest. Some groups used video film, some started with camera work, and some started with pupils talking about their own impressions of the school. Gradually, all moved on to tour the school and all but one covered some camera work.

In the subsequent debriefing (which was not joined by the teacher), I raised a number of basic questions about the sharing of work between pupils and students in the group; the different styles and strategies adopted by different groups; the attitudes of pupils and students and how they were expressed; group relationships and how groups chose to arrange themselves physically; the timing and basic organisation (coverage of material versus pupil learning); who took responsibility for the whole class as well as the individual group; how much they had learnt about pupils' abilities; and the procedure of packing up. The most important issue emerged as a result of a question about *how* each student group went about facilitating the pupils' practical knowledge and understanding of the workings of the cameras. It was clear that some groups had been taught and told while others had been more actively involved in learning. Encouragingly, individual students could say of themselves that they had done too much telling. In later sessions some debriefing was done by students of each other, thus using the 'team' situation as described in Chapter 7.

There was also a very useful debriefing by TP. She had herself experienced similar sorts of debriefing from me in the first term of her own course as part of the Double Focus technique described in Chapter 10, and was very confident about the sort of processes expected of her. Fortunately, her view was from inside the school. In this respect she provided some, but not all, of what the class teacher might have offered. She was able to cast the pupils' behaviour in a new light, declaring that the individual pupils she had watched had responded very differently from 'usual' (that is, how she had seen them around the school). She was also able to remind the students about the procedures of the school for written work and homework. These had changed to some extent since my term's exchange.

Perhaps the final comments on the first visit should be left with a student:

> The pupils remembered us from the previous weeks, yet at first seemed a little restrained. After we had introduced the project, however, they seemed more attentive and became quite interested. We had to do most of the talking and gave

lots of information without much feedback from them.

When the roles were changed and they showed us round the school, their attitudes changed too. They were put in the position of knowing everything, and they responded to the task very well.

One of the good things was that they worked as a group rather than individuals . . . . We got the most response when we gave them responsibility . . . . If we had dominated the lesson too much we would not have gained any insight into their characters, attitudes and abilities.

From the knowledge we gained of their ability we have had to adjust the scheme of work and week two lesson plan. They are slow to pick up information . . . .(HW)

Subsequent visits

As might be expected, the work in weeks two to six gathered momentum. By the second week, the pupils were already beginning to be the envy of their peers for what was widely perceived as a very prestigious project. This in turn caused groups to take on new images of themselves, although, of course, not all pupils were equally enthusiastic.

During these weeks the pupils learnt that what was required was hard work, but that this did show results. They also learnt that they could develop a different working relationship with their 'teachers'. The fact that these were known to be students led to the breaking down of some inhibiting barriers as they began to work together against two common enemies – time, and some appalling weather.

As time went on, too, the students learnt a number of predictable lessons from which I had refused to let myself shield them. Many of these emerged as the students talked together about their impressions of each other and the pupils. They learnt about the tensions between the needs of plenty of time for experiential learning and the process model on the one hand, and the need to cover the ground fast and to have something to show at the end on the other. They learnt of some of the snags of not checking equipment beforehand. They learnt to read pupils' body language and not to allow their own to give the wrong messages. They learnt the use of space in rooms and how to change the physical details in order to create different moods, and foster different kinds of learning. They learnt the importance of standing back and letting the pupils do the planning and the practical work, and even letting them learn from their own mistakes, and they learnt the importance of observing both pupils and each other while standing back.

At week five I asked for a statement from every student on what they had learnt so far. The issues which figured most prominently were:

— the value of the sort of stimulus that video work can offer
— the need always to have a 'fall-back' position
— the fact that practical work of this kind can involve all pupils in a group no matter what their ability
— the value of informal as well as formal relationships, and the fact that, properly handled, this is not a problem with this age-group

— the value of the cooperative skill of group work
— the importance of pupils being allowed to express their own feelings, reactions, attitudes in a clear and well communicated way
— the importance of oral skills (both pupils' and teacher's).

At about week five, too, I learnt that there had not been enough discussion in either the student or the pupil groups of the idea of audience for the videos. This also related to the problem of how to handle the school image. Although pupils were ready to be critical of school orally, they seemed to feel the pressure to present a balanced or even positive view of the school on film. Though this loyalty was commendable in one way, the possibilities had been lost of using the filming more imaginatively and for a range of different audiences. But there were some successes too, including changed attitudes. One whole group of pupils volunteered to arrive early before the beginning of the school day in order to film a close-questioning interview with the headmaster, in which the pupils asked some sharp questions and the head found himself playing the urbane diplomat.

The last visit

The plan for the final week was that each group should meet to start with, view and discuss its own video, prepare a group statement as an introduction to it, and decide what kind of questions to have in mind while watching the other films. Following this, the five films, all about 15 minutes long, were to be shown in an order the students had predetermined, and which took account of break-time. During the morning, one student was to hold the fort at the 'front' and all the others were to help from the sides.

In the event, the first section went off smoothly, but without the work being fully exploited because the students had not thought the work through in enough detail. Thus, the unearthing of the pupils' own perceptions of what they had learnt was done by experienced teachers who had come to watch.

Nevertheless, there was much that was learnt here by all involved, as the following perspectives upon the project show.

Some perspectives on the project

From the students

It seems only right to begin with extracts from four of the students' critical reviews of this work. They are chosen as representing a range of views, but all make comments in their own way about the project's value for them and for the pupils. One of the clearest patterns to emerge is that of the changes of attitude wrought in these disaffected pupils by the work – and, of course, by the staff-student ratio.

> Whenever we spent the lessons outside with cameras and actually began filming, their whole attitude changed. They became keen and willing to discuss the

problems that arose, which they initially ignored in the classroom. It is a mistake, however, to totally ignore the pupils' problems with reading and writing. Therefore, to encourage them to put down their ideas on paper, we supplied them the project's special sheets. When we supervised their writing in class they wrote very little even on the sheets we provided, but when we set the task of planning the following session for homework, the difference was noticeable. In her homework Tessa's ideas are much clearer and better thought out ... she has begun to visualise how her ideas can be translated from paper on to the screen, which is very good especially considering her apprehensiveness at the beginning of the project. She has listened to instructions and has added her own ideas.

Thus, from this instance it is evident that we must provide a good stimulus if we wish to encourage pupils to write down their ideas. This is even more important for those with lesser ability. The pupils' attitude to being on film showed the most marked improvement of all. In the first few weeks they lacked confidence, but this grew enormously. The main reason for this was that they realised that the responsibility was given to them. (ST)

Some reviews concentrated more on the student's own role:

My input was mostly concentrated on the discussion sessions in the lessons. My two colleagues and I shared the teaching responsibilities well ... and I think I benefited enormously from their criticism and praise. (RN)

Some saw the potential of the work for pupils, for students, and for future planning. This led to some valuable reflection.

We were given great insight into the possibilities of incorporating practical work into this subject. With greater flexibility of time all aspects of English work could have arisen naturally as part of the project ....

The other major achievement which I feel I have made is the progression of my observation skills. Working as a team has enabled me to spend time observing the pupils and seeing how they react to things said and done by a teacher. Also seeing how other teachers manage, motivate and encourage a group of pupils has made me look more critically at my own teaching methods.

More knowledge about how much of the discussion should come from me and how much should come from the pupils would have helped initially, although this was gained as I got to know the pupils better ....

The pupils, I feel, gained a lot and achieved an enormous amount from this project .... (BS)

Some saw a range of benefits that lurked beneath the surface of the more obvious ones.

During our previous experiences in school, while on teaching practice, we had been in sole charge of a class. It was therefore a strange experience to be working as a trio. At first we felt uneasy and uncomfortable in each other's presence. Often one of us was not used in the teaching situation, but instead of doing nothing the 'spare' teacher was able to make notes on both the pupils and ourselves. The feedback after the lesson was therefore of greater relevance and this wider view of the lesson was helpful in the preparation for the following week.

I feel strongly that the success of this project was not the completion of a video but the development and achievements of the pupils. The status of this group of low ability and/or disaffected pupils has clearly risen in the eyes of their peers and teachers. All the pupils developed during the six weeks. Marla was the least interested in the group but we exploited her interest in making the opening titles during her art lesson . . . . The main lesson I have learnt is always to have a back-up plan no matter how safe you think your original plans. This project has prompted me to rethink how I could approach my next teaching practice, looking at areas such as the room lay-out, group work and my own attitude and relationship with pupils. I have learnt not to underestimate the abilities of the less able, and that when given responsibility for something they can be motivated to work hard. (WH)

From the pupils

The following extracts are from the work of five pupils and were written after the completion of the project. (One pupil wrote six sides.) The class teacher was not part of the project but usefully acted as an audience for their writing. Particularly illuminating are the comments on the students and the response to them that this reveals; the tolerance of the pupils over the mistakes made by the students, and the willingness to continue with the work despite this; and their awareness of the processes they were undergoing.

Personal report on film-making

The first few weeks were really talking about how we should go about making the video. There was alot (sic) of buttons to remember and before you could start filming you would have to change the light sensor and wind the film on. It was organised very well with very few mistakes. They only made two real blunders, the first being that we didn't know that every time you switch the recorder off it automatically rewound. The second problem was that after three weeks of filming one of the students took the video home and someone in the household recorded over it with some inferior piece of television. The man who recorded over this should be put down. This meant that we had to fit all our takes into three weeks, guess what? We done it. (KH)

What I learned from the experience

This video was a joint effort and one of the things I learned from it was that when all the ideas are put together we can make one really good video with everybodies best ideas. I think the teachers went away thinking that they had done themselves proud by pulling together a good video, so they learned something too. (DY)

I learned a great deal from my experience with the group I was in, although I was the only girl who turned up. I thoroughly enjoyed myself and I'd do it again for the simple fact once we worked as a team it felt good and things were being done. The student teachers we worked with were very helpful and encouraging. They praised you when you needed it and they made you overcome your shyness whilst in front of the camera. (MI)

I learnt that I don't have to do all my school work on paper. I think I got better results from filming. (YZ)

Some people thought it was boring but I thought it good fun. We had a good laugh with the students and I think they would make good teachers. We didn't have much time really six weeks wasn't very long but at the end it turned all right I was pleased with it and so was the students and that all what counts (sic). (TF)

The experience we got from the lessons was of course we learned how to use a camera. But also how to react to talking on your own to a camera. It was hard at first because the camera didn't answer you back and it couldn't laugh at you if you did something wrong. I hate talking to anyone face to face and really at the end of it all you was talking to the whole class. And it gave us a good chance to say what we thought of school. But it wasn't the real truth. I don't think I would like to do it every week, it was very hard work and made you think about what you were doing. (DR)

If these comments indicate the kind of attitudes and awareness of the pupils, the following comments provide a more dispassionate and very useful view.

From the TP student

To my mind one of the most striking results of the project (although perhaps the most predictable) were the changing relationships between teachers and pupils, and between pupils themselves.... Watching one group in particular, the barriers between individuals crumbled faster as time ran out, until, in the final day of filming, the five people concerned were able to discuss their videos almost as equals. Interestingly, the video had shown signs of being very teacher-directed but on this final day the pupils definitely took over. The change in pupil/teacher relationships was facilitated by a change in environment. Filming proved an excellent way of taking English work outside the confines of the classroom, without turning this departure into a 'treat'.

I would have been surprised, given the circumstances, if the pupils had failed to respond positively to the work and in fact only a few individuals did not join in the general enthusiasm for the project. Certainly the group that I watched had become so caught up in what they were doing by the final week that they needed very little direction and no urging to work. The three committed members of the group produced very adequate written homework which they had discussed in their own time before presenting it to the teachers.

What does interest me is the fact that there were two individuals in the group who did not respond to the project. I do not know enough of either of these pupils to hazard a guess as to why this should have been so....

From the answers solicited by one of the English staff in the final session, it was apparent that at least some of the pupils were aware of the benefits of such a project where it concerned their learning. It would have been interesting to explore this understanding earlier....

I thought that the project proved very successful. It was certainly fascinating to watch in operation. (TP)

Some reflections

Next time

The following are extracts from some resolutions I made for the re-run of the project.

> The basic plan of this work will need to be salvaged, but the balance of time must be altered. The planning of schemes of work and lessons will be tackled as before since this approach to planning has proved the best way yet encountered of teaching students about preparation. This aspect of the work would be worth investigating more closely next time.
>
> The detailed replanning will need to include more time in school, some of which can be used for the debriefing of pupils as advised by TP. The issues about awareness of audience and purpose must be tackled from the beginning of the first term and will be monitored throughout the second term also.
>
> Most of all, additional time is going to have to be put in on working with the school staff on their role and contribution. This is going to involve considerable diplomacy, and can perhaps best be approached as a plea for help.

The role of the school staff

Undeniably, throughout the project in school, all those involved except the pupils came up against some frustrations or a sense of loss because of the inability to share these experiences with the class teacher. This would have been even worse had the TP student not been there.

It would seem prudent, then, to involve the teacher in the first term's work in college. This would mean involvement in the preparation of the students for the school work. This would ensure that by the time the second term is reached all parties will have been more used to working on the same topics. It will also be necessary to ask the teacher to stay throughout the lessons and to contribute to the debriefing. This may be difficult to timetable, but should not be impossible. By working with the tutor in both the observation and the debriefing, it may be possible to bring the teacher to see some value to himself, as well as his undoubted value to the students, in his contributions.

Other possible adaptations

Although this work had in fact been carried out with BEd secondary students and disaffected fourth years, it would be equally possible to site it in the top end of the primary school. (All filming could be done with the aid of tripods thus removing any potential problems about holding heavy cameras.) Indeed, in some ways, a top age junior class would get at least as much or probably more out of such an exercise. The skills and capacities which could be fostered are virtually endless. Further, it could be conducted by primary or secondary BEd or (if there were time) PGCE students. But as part of this work, the tradition of learning together and along with the students needs to be established so that students are not seen as a spare pair of hands, and students accompanied by a tutor are not seen as an absolute release for the teacher.

10. Developing a Double Focus: Teaching and Learning to Teach in Tandem

Summary

- Double Focus: the practice and its theory
  — the main action
  — the centrality of reflection
- The participants' perspectives
  — the practical setting
  — early reactions
  — reflection seen as central
  — moments of insight
  — some real learning from practice
  — the teacher's role
  — seeing beyond the model
- Reflections upon the technique
  — how it relates to other approaches
  — its limitations
  — its particular contributions
- The practical implications
  — for teachers
  — for tutors
  — for students

Introduction

During training and after it, the successful teacher frequently calls upon two levels of awareness. He has, concomitantly, to be a teacher and to learn to be one. Such a double focus demands from the recruit new dispositions, skills, and understanding. The Double Focus technique described below illustrates the possibilities of fostering these, in a sheltered arena, from the very beginning of the initial training course.

This particular version of school experience involves a tutor, and up to 16 students, working regularly together in one classroom with any normal sized class and their teacher. The experience, embedded in discussion, fuelled by reading and reflection, and operating on a problem-solving basis, has proved to be a fruitful means of eroding the barriers between training institutions and schools, and between theory and practice. Most importantly, it is one way of helping students to recognise and grapple with some of the deeper aspects of learning and teaching. In this respect it might well have something to offer to training in other professional fields, and can certainly be used in both primary and secondary schools, with both BEd and PGCE students. It is currently in use in year one of the Primary BEd at West London Institute.

Double Focus: the practice and its theory

The main action

The central actions of the Double Focus technique are perhaps best described via metaphors drawn from drama. The cast involves an entire education group, a full and unpurged class of pupils, a teacher, and a tutor. The setting is the normal school classroom, and the normal timetable and regular lesson for the class. In the case of secondary students, the selection of the lesson might be made deliberately to exclude the students' main subjects, since this can help them to distance themselves from the content of the lesson. The routines, rituals, and layout of the classroom are not disturbed, but additional chairs are available among the pupils, perhaps on the basis of one student to two pupils where possible (but one to one, or one to three, works equally as well), and seating will be in groups or whatever is the normal arrangement, with five or six pupils to two or three students. The students are introduced and always referred to as teachers. The duration of the entire work is equivalent to about one full day (where half a day is spent in school, and up to half of the day following in college). The amount of time spent in the classroom is one hour, or one lesson's length. The day equivalent would be one-fifth of the students' normal week for about four or five weeks in the period leading up to the first (one or two) teaching practice(s).

The central action involves every character present fulfilling both a teaching and a learning role, within his or her normal sphere of operation. The task of the teacher is, predominantly, to teach the class (enable them to learn), but with an eye to helping the students to learn, and to learning from the situation himself. The role of the tutor is to teach the students (enable them to learn), but with an eye to the pupils' learning also, and to learn from the situation himself. This technique can profitably be varied once the tutor becomes familiar with the class, by teacher and tutor reversing the roles.

The pupils' role is to learn from (or with) the teacher, to be helped where appropriate by the tutor and the students, and to teach them much also. The role of the student is to learn, at the same time, to teach and to learn to teach, by adopting an enquiry-oriented approach to all that happens, by setting out to focus on a particular agreed set of issues, and by seeking to challenge theory with practice and practice with theory, in order to begin to formulate a personal theory. The student will often involve herself in the pupils' work, where appropriate and as directed by the teacher, but she will also begin to learn to detach herself enough to enable the pupils to take responsibility for their own work.

Thus, all of the adults involved are continuously and consciously employing a double focus on teaching and learning to teach, and that double focus is, in a sense, personified by the teacher and tutor. For this reason it seems applicable to refer to this as the Double Focus technique, although in doing so, there is no wish to undervalue the multiplicity of perspectives implicit in such methods.

The centrality of reflection

The other essential to the drama is that it involves at least six kinds of Act, all directed at bringing reflection to bear on practice in a carefully sequenced order. First, of course, comes the Act involving detailed preparation, and including four scenes: for tutor and teacher together; for tutor and students together; for teacher and pupils together; and for all adult participants together (albeit briefly, perhaps just prior to the lesson). This must be followed by the Second Act – about an hour or so in class. (The time for this central activity is deliberately relatively brief simply because of the amount of concentration needed, and because of the impossibility of a useful and thorough debriefing of anything longer.)

The Third Act, an immediate follow-up discussion during the other hour or so in school, would normally include all the adults involved, together with some feedback where possible from the pupils. The Fourth Act takes place on the evening of the day in school, when a diary or log of the day's events is completed and personal reflections upon them are captured, and when associated reading, related to the work in terms of issues and methodology, is carried out. (The reading assignment is usually to be completed after the written impressions, so that personal reactions are captured before new perspectives are brought to bear on the student's thinking.)

Fifth, there is then a more distanced, critical review and exploration of the issues arising (about the educational means and ends and investigation itself) on the day following in a college-based seminar. The physical location of this work away from the school can be important at this point, in order to provide a distanced perspective, but this is not in order to exclude the further contribution of the teacher, and indeed, it is regarded as desirable that all the adult participants again be present. Finally, and deliberately at some remove in time and place from this block of work, the student, using her log and notes made from readings and seminars, attempts to chart her own development in terms of ideas, knowledge, skills, and capacities across the five or so weeks of this work. This brief report, which can be used to assess the student's work, together with relevant appended working papers, is then responded to in writing, individually, by the tutor.

What, then, is involved in the main detail of each Act, and how does it promote reflection?

Clearly, the preparation stage must involve negotiation between teacher and tutor, both at a philosophical level in terms of what students should be taught and when (and whether the Double Focus technique is the best means), and in terms of the practical constraints of the classroom situation and the pupils' own development. In particular, care must be taken, in planning, that work which is designed to help the students does not conflict with pupils' interests.

The preparation necessary between the teacher and his class will vary depending upon the age of the class and the intentions of the teacher for the particular lesson to be observed. An enterprising teacher may well use the occasions to help pupils relate to adults. In one particularly successful case, the teacher turned the tables on the students by preparing the pupils to be the experts in the particular activity. Certainly, some special thought also needs to be given to the very first occasion on which students and pupils meet, and time must be allowed for them to get to know each other.

The preparation with the students (which might involve teacher plus tutor, or just tutor) concerns itself at first with establishing clearly what roles the students will play:

(a) as teachers, working with pupils in class in support of the teacher
(b) as students of teaching and learning, focusing on an aspect, or aspects, on which they will reflect in depth both during and after the lesson.

This involves the students being briefed by the teacher at some point about methods and content, and by the tutor about observation itself, about the issues under consideration, and about reflection.

Thus, the students will enter the classroom with agreed and shared areas of enquiry, and a clear idea of how and when to cooperate with the teacher, and how and when to turn their attention to the agreed learning issues. Examples of such issues might include a consideration of what is involved in teaching or in learning on that particular occasion, or might be a more specific exploration of the place of writing in learning, or of issues related to multiculturalism or second language learning. But they will also be alerted to watch for the unexpected.

During their work in the classroom, students help pupils as necessary, and when they are not needed, record information about the pupils and their work. This very recording itself, of course, demands reflection and lays the basis for further discussion. Figure 4 shows the kind of sheets designed to assist this process.

Sheet 1 (side 1):
(For use while the teacher works with the whole class: the beginning and end of the lesson.)

You are not here to model the master teacher. You are not being shown a demonstration of exactly how *you* should teach *your* pupils. That is for you to decide as the course proceeds. You are here to make a start towards it by beginning to think about what is really involved in the activities of teaching and learning. Use this sheet (both sides) to help you think about what is involved in this lesson. Distance yourself from the content, think critically about the activities of teacher and pupils. Make brief notes on this sheet for your own use in later discussions. Do not write detailed notes about the events of the lesson. Write as little as possible to help you remember the key things you noticed.

1. How is the lesson introduced. Why?

2. What is the pupils' main task? How was it introduced? Why?

3. What are the main problems for the pupils near you as they listen to the teacher?

4. How does the teacher help to sustain their concentration?

5. What examples are there of interruptions external to the lesson? What would *you* have done about them?

6. What examples are there of interruptions internal to the lesson? Why? What would you have done?

7. What examples are there of teacher anticipating and deflecting problems?

8. At what point were resources distributed? Why?

9. How was the lesson drawn to a close?

10. Any other thoughts?

Sheet 1 (side 2)
(For use while pupils carry our group work and written tasks.)
NB. When referring to an individual pupil use first names only.

Remain beside your pupil(s), and answer questions 1 and 2, but also observe answers to 3. Keep yourself busy writing while actually observing. Do NOT involve yourself in the pupils' work at the start of it. They might try to get you to do it for them, but that is NOT your role. Do not interrupt pupils while they work, wait until they have finished or seek specific help. The more quickly you look busy the more quickly they will settle.

1. What did you notice about the questions the teacher asked at the start of the lesson?

> 2. What were your impressions of the pupils' responses?
>
> 3. What do you observe about your pupils' group as they begin to discuss?
>
> 4. What do you observe about your pupil as s/he begins to write:
>   — starting rituals?
>
>   — concentration span?
>
>   — particular difficulties?
>
>   — timing and reasons for interruption of writing?
>
>   — amount of written work produced in length of time?
>
>   — quality of it?
>
>   — other thoughts.

Figure 4: Observation tasks

By means of schedules like these and on-the-spot guidance of the tutor, the students are constantly alerted to the need to switch from teaching to learning, or to attempt both together, and so are encouraged, from the beginning, to think and act at the same time. Both the tutor and the teacher work freely around the class among the pupils and students. Either will address the 'teachers' sitting among the class, perhaps drawing attention to a key point. (Learning *to see* is a part of their training which is not always given much attention.) The teacher's main focus is upon the pupils, however.

The tutor's role throughout is to help improve students' practice, and observation, and their reflection upon both. The tutor will draw attention to key incidents, by acting like a third eye and ear, helping students to see, hear, and reflect upon what they might otherwise miss, and developing these capacities in them. In this way, the tutor leads the students to consider the expected and the unexpected factors of the classroom, and seeks to help them to develop their thinking, and practice, to refine their judgements and decision-making, and to consider their own preferred modes of operation and associated rationales.

The pupils are taught to listen selectively when they are addressed and to ignore comments addressed only to the 'teachers' sitting among them. They are usually remarkably quick to develop this capacity. Some shorthand jargon naturally evolves among the adults also, which enables attention to be drawn to certain occurrences without making pupils self-conscious.

The importance of the immediate debriefing is that it captures and allows for exchange of immediate reactions, ideas, and knowledge, and will reveal the multiple perspectives involved in perceiving, interpreting, recording, and decision-making. Vital background information to an incident, from the teacher, can also enlighten understanding of motives and intentions. A consideration of the unexpected versus the planned can also prove rewarding.

The tutor's task here, and in the next day's follow-up, is to enable students to exhume or create and refine their own theories of action by means of reflection and deliberation. This involves observations, reactions, interpretations, criticism, and analysis being placed side by side with a range of theoretical perspectives which students are developing for themselves and gaining from their previous evening's reading.

It is a natural part of this work that it emphasises the process of learning in the school classroom, and sees learning in terms of processes. It can also draw the student to see a link between approaches to learning in the school and on her own course. As the work begins to gather momentum, areas of shared interest begin to be negotiated between all the adults involved, and there is genuinely fresh learning in it for everyone.

The participants' perspectives

By far the best way of giving a flavour of the excitement involved in this form of learning is to present the following perspectives.

The practical setting

The comments below are taken from work in a 1200-strong community school in outer London, which reflected the local community in containing about a 70 per cent Asian population, and which catered for the 11 to 18 age-range. Here, 16 PGCE secondary students shared the experience of what became known as a core lesson across five weeks. The lesson lasted one hour and was followed by one hour's follow-up, with the teacher involved. The first three of the four lessons were with Ms C, an experienced history teacher, who took a first-year class in combined humanities (CHums) which included history, geography, and RE. The class contained 28 pupils, in a normal classroom, and the desks were set out in groups, with the students provided with seats among the groups. The theme for that part of term was 'Individuality'. The fourth week saw us sharing a lesson in drama with Miss P, the coordinator of creative arts and a very experienced drama teacher, and a third year of 18 pupils who were exploring the idea of 'Celebration' as part of a creative arts programme which included lessons in creative writing, drama, and music. The lesson was a practical one, held not in a classroom, but in a rather overused lounge area in the Youth Block.

Early reactions

The very first of these core lessons took place two days after the students had

Developing a Double Focus 151

arrived and registered for their course. The school had been back from the summer holidays for seven working days and the first-year class were still very new to Ms C and to each other. However, because one of the points about CHums is that the same teacher takes all aspects of it, the class had actually met five times already. The work was, therefore, already under way, the theme had been introduced, the pupils were prepared for their visitors, and had ready an identity-swopping exercise for the first five minutes of the first shared lesson. (This was the only respect in which their programme was different in content from all four other first-year groups.) By the second week the students as well as the pupils were old hands, as we see in the following comment from GM (a PE student with English subsidiary).

> The whole group of trainee teachers was dispersed at different tables throughout the first-year class of 28 pupils.
> I am sitting at a table with five kids and two other 'teachers', in between a young Asian girl called Mandi and a white girl called Sara. (GM)

The pupils' reactions to the situation were captured by RP (RE with English subsidiary) in a comment which also reveals his not uncommon underlying needs and anxieties.

> The most pleasing thing about the visit was the way in which the children immediately accepted our presence, and, in many cases if not all, ignored it unless told not to. Their attitude made me feel at ease – it was not me who put them at ease, but they who made me feel comfortable . . . . It was nice when one of the girls, Rochel, with whom I'd been working, ran past me as I was leaving, and took time out to say goodbye. (RP)

This was also commented on by JW (PE and geography) in his reflection on the third-year drama lesson in which the pupils were working out an improvisation in three groups.

> One of the most notable features of the lesson was how uninhibited the pupils were, especially with us watching. (JW)

Reflection seen as central

Observation was not of course the only activity required of students. They also worked with the pupils and proved very ready to see that reflection and debriefing in the follow-up were both a necessary and a complementary activity to that in the classroom. Here TM (PE and English) makes the point:

> The most rewarding aspect of the day was the core lesson and the immediate follow-up. I never realised the full role of the teacher in terms of preparation, and now it seems obvious . . . .
> We noted the idea of key stages in the lesson. It seems a vital part of lesson planning. I'd forgotten how immature 11 year olds are and how the teacher has to cope with it. Ms C is very patient and her use of language is interesting to observe. (TM)

And:

> The core lesson again proved a valuable insight into this week's theme 'What is teaching?' There is no right answer to this question . . . . Ms C showed that a teacher has many roles to play in one lesson. Our first visit to our main subject revealed further roles. (GM)

Moments of insight

Indeed, this particular lesson, the third and last one with Ms C and her first year, proved to be, as was intended, the most thought-provoking. The issue for the students was 'What is learning?' and a sheet (coded DF 13) had been prepared for the students to help them look at and think about various aspects of learning while pupils were working alone. The description of the lesson is taken up by NB (whose subjects were English with history) at the point where, after leading a discussion about things which made us all afraid, Ms C collected some data on the board and set pupils off to make a group pictogram to illustrate it. The class had discussed pictograms in a previous lesson, and were due later to do further work on data processing. They therefore knew (perhaps better than the students) what the end-product should be like. Their problem was that Ms C had deliberately not told them how to set about organising their group. To make matters more difficult, the students had not been briefed about this part of the lesson either.

> We were given no information as to how the task should be done. We had no 'stars' in our group and consequently the scene was one of bewilderment. None of the pupils wanted to take the initiative and looked at us for guidance. Since we were unaware how far we were meant to get involved with 'their' work, we held back – stalemate! In growing desperation we set too (sic) with scissors and card and allocated children to draw various symbols. About this time the lesson ended.
>
> Instead of an attempt at learning, it became a race against time. We had plenty of bewilderment, but, unfortunately, it became an end in itself rather than the beginning of learning.
>
> In the follow-up, however, several points became apparent that I hadn't considered at the time of the lesson but can now see as crucial to learning. Clearly the ball had been very much in the children's court. This was something I was unprepared for. Ms C's previous (two) lessons had been heavily teacher-dominated (I felt) and I found it hard to imagine her 'letting the children go'. Thus, in this lesson, I thought I must have missed something rather than concentrating on the fact that the children were meant to learn for themselves.
>
> This, then, was a practical example of how answers must be drawn from pupils rather than given to them . . . . Ms C wasn't going to tell the groups how to do it. One group that further questioned her had the problem reset in different terms, but not solved for them. The children were learning social skills, interaction, the need for compromise. They perhaps became more aware that most people are good at something and that pooling people's resources creates better quality products.
>
> The teacher's role in learning of this nature is as a resource, therefore. Ms C provided all the necessary materials, collected the necessary information, and was at hand at all times to help, but did very little telling . . . .
>
> This, then, was a lesson where pupils learnt how to learn. There were no facts to

digest. . . . The children were actually involved in working with each other, and in this instance, the process of learning was more important than the actual product produced. This fact will not stop the children gaining satisfaction from their finished work, however.

This way of learning was quite new to me. All I can remember of my own school days was being 'taught' by teacher. . . . but I can see how it complements the more formal teaching approach that I'm used to. Each has relevance to pupil development, one more inclined to social skills, the other to academic achievement. Together they should provide a balanced education. (NB)

The pace and style of this diary extract neatly capture the atmosphere, the emotions and the pressures felt by the students, together with their reservations about the activity, and provides an interesting chart and flavour of the inevitably jerky progress towards new understanding. Its sharply focused critical thinking was typical of some of the best reactions to this work in both oral and written reflections. For example, JW's (PE and history) reaction was similar, though he went on to draw some more practical conclusions:

Today Ms C allowed us to be more involved and to help the pupils in their task of making a pictogram . . . . For this reason the lesson seemed to fly by, and it wasn't until the follow-up that it became really clear what the pupils were doing . . . .

Ms C made this lesson a problem-solving one for each group of pupils . . . .

When planning a lesson of this kind it is important for teacher to think in terms of supplying what is needed for the task, and then wait for the pupils to ask for help . . . . Teaching should be about setting up situations in which the pupils have to solve problems, which helps them to learn how to learn. (JW)

Perhaps the only additional step that he did not take here was seeing that he too was involved in the same kind of activity at his own level.

That this was not an isolated case of insight was shown also by AI (RE and history) who, in a more general reflection on what she had learnt by week three, wrote:

At this point what I have learnt most is that being a teacher involves not just acquiring skills, ie to give clear instructions etc, although that is important, but rather that it is the teacher's job to facilitate pupils' learning. At this point the question: 'What is teaching?' becomes redundant. It is rather a question of learning and of how the teacher can facilitate it. (AI)

Some real learning from practice

One final example from JD (English and history) shows how far information, experience, and reflection can lead to real learning. Of the same pictogram lesson, he wrote, somewhat lyrically and partly with tongue-in-cheek, but nonetheless with considerable insight:

Our group groped away at it for the rest of the lesson – didn't seem to get much done. Meanwhile we groped away at DF 13, and got less done than they did. We were all absorbed by the practical problems they were facing up to.

Back in the debriefing room Dr Fish asked Ms C the burning question: 'What was the point of all that?' Unfortunately, WE were supposed to answer it. Long

> silence. At last Robert (RP) suggested that the children were learning to work in groups, as a team. We still tried to justify it in terms of content. 'They were learning to translate material from one medium to another. 'They were learning to put down on paper abstract concepts.' In short we all felt that several acres of expensive coloured paper had been consumed to no apparent purpose. But then we came to realise – they had been 'doing', a more fertile type of learning but with less polished appearance – experimenting, making mistakes, finding their own ways .... The purpose of the lesson had been to facilitate this ....
>
> I have been forced to examine (to see) my own strong PRODUCER/CONTENT (sic) prejudices and admit that I failed to spot them through the sessions on 'What is teaching?' despite all the emphasis on doing. (JD)

The gracefully revealed honesty about the process of his own learning and thinking, with its failures as well as its successes, and the fearless way in which he analysed the group's mixed reactions during the debriefing, are both indicative of the very positive atmosphere which develops in a group that works as closely together as this experience requires. This too, of course, is a major means of bringing them to consider what learning is like from the inside, and the supportive and secure atmosphere needed for it. This group were quick to grasp the idea that mistakes are a very useful starting point for learning.

The teacher's role

Lest it should seem that all of the insights came from Ms C's core lessons, here is a comment from JW about Miss P's drama:

> The teacher's role in this lesson was to press forward the logic of what was being learnt and to keep things going. Miss P made sure that the task was open-ended . . . but at the same time she kept the lesson structured.
>
> Miss P was not speaking most of the time, but instead she observed each group and held back, waiting for the right moment to go in and help. It is important for the teacher to use within the lessons the ideas the pupils bring. (JW)

The first point was also noted by BT (PE and English). From it she drew a conclusion which often does not occur to students until the end of their first practice:

> Miss P didn't always speak. She often observed silently for a while. Holding back can sometimes be one of the greatest skills of a teacher. (BT)

None of these insights would have come to students sitting in lectures in college, not even in lectures on these topics. Neither would they have come from sustained school experience alone, when the pressures of the daily task often preclude any lengthy reflection, and certainly do not allow for much in the way of a shared analysis with peers. This approach seems to appeal to students because it recognises and harnesses their own intellectual skills, and shows some of the more intellectual challenges of teaching from the beginning of the course. Thus, while it does not ignore the early need for the development of some basic classroom skills, it looks beyond them to a less simplistic concept of what teaching is about.

Seeing beyond the model

Finally, it should not be supposed that these students were gullible and passive receivers of these experiences, ready to take as a model the first teacher they observed in detail. Indeed, the later reflection sessions are geared to extrapolate beyond what they have seen, and to get them to consider their own values, capacities, preferences, knowledge, and skills. The following three examples show this in action.

> I must add that I feel that Ms C does tend to treat her first-year class too much like babies. But she does get the required results.
> Also, through her I have seen the pastoral side of teaching. She has discreetly made us aware of children's personal problems as well as the caution that must be displayed when dealing with a multicultural class. (BT)

> Ms C's style is to allow five minutes and then to wander among the children, looking at what they have written and answering questions. This is not a style I would choose to adopt. Personally, if I were a pupil I would either resent this intrusion . . . or would use it as an excuse for asking redundant questions, time-wasting etc.
> To my mind, this kind of 'fussing' by teacher seems to be to no purpose. Indeed, it may well disturb an otherwise concentrated period of working. (NB)

> Ms C claims that first years need a sense of security, so should not be pushed too hard in the first couple of weeks. If the tasks set are hard, continued failure will undermine a child's confidence. However I am uneasy about this. (JS)

Clearly some of these comments were to suffer revision in the light of the students' own practice, but some points were valid.

For those whose curiosity extends to wondering about the reactions of the other three groups of participants, the following comments must be made.

The reactions of the pupils involved were mainly that they enjoyed meeting and working with 'their' teachers. Indeed, a number openly missed the students when they left. Many also said that having a teacher by your side when you needed it, instead of having to wait for ages, perhaps with your hand up, was really helpful. Ms C reported that for some weeks afterwards the pupils continued to ask after their visitors.

The reactions of the two members of staff involved were that they thoroughly enjoyed the work, and appreciated the amount that they got out of being made to think through in detail both what they were going to do, and what they had done. They also admitted to some surprise on occasions at some of the motives and even educational thinking that had been attributed to them, when they felt that they had 'only acted automatically'. The other most striking comment was about the feeling of redundancy that arose because other help from the students was immediately on hand.

As the tutor involved, my main reactions will already have emerged. I find it stimulating (because there is always so much to learn), demanding (especially at the preparation level), and extremely rewarding when students share the kind of thinking cited above. For me it brings out the essential nature of what teacher training should provide – an emphasis on the learner learning, rather than the teacher teaching. And it brings it out at student level as well as pupil level.

Reflections upon the technique

What, then, is the value of this technique and what is its contribution to training?

How it relates to other approaches

Double Focus technique is different in at least seven major ways from other intermittent experience. First, it avoids being a 'total immersion' method, while at the same time it does give students the feel of the complexity of the classroom, and sheltered experiences of working with pupils. Second, it achieves this while countering the dangers of the apprenticeship model, by involving more than one qualified professional in the classroom. Thus, it neither resembles teaching practice nor 'sitting with Nellie'.

Third, and more importantly, unlike any other approach, it features a teacher centre stage, *together* with a tutor, thus establishing a genuine partnership, and allowing the strengths and contributions of both the training institution and the school to be used together in a complementary rather than a competitive approach to training. Fourth, because of this, although it is not of itself a version of triangulation (the enquiry method which draws upon the perspective of three people in investigating classrooms), it certainly establishes and fosters relationships which could develop into a triangulation approach to teaching practice, and into a cooperative approach to the selection of intending teachers.

Fifth, it allows for an exceptional staff/student ratio, unlike most labour-intensive versions of school experience, and provides a reasonable sized discussion group. Further, unlike other versions, it establishes in the students' minds from the beginning of the course the fact that they are teachers and learners of teaching simultaneously, and uses this in preparing them for a reflective teaching practice and subsequent professional life. Finally, and perhaps most importantly, because of its enquiry approach it allows the students to find out for themselves what sort of people they are and what they might particularly bring to teaching, as well as allowing them to discover what teaching demands. And it does so in a sheltered environment. It is thus a good example of a practicum.

So what, then, are some of the limitations of the Double Focus technique?

Its limitations

Like all innovative methods, it is liable to become distorted through misunderstanding. A too eager teacher, anxious to involve the students in the lesson itself, to the exclusion of allowing them time to distance themselves, and to the exclusion of the tutor's role, can easily turn the proceedings into a kind of total immersion, where double focus is lost in favour of simply 'experiencing teaching'. (This can be the result of too limited preparation, particularly between the tutor and teacher, and of their not really sharing the problem-oriented approach to teaching and training for teaching.) Similarly, an overanxious tutor, keen to defer to the school on its own territory, can allow a senior teacher to take over the organisation of the programme and find himself working with those who adopt an apprenticeship model, either by excluding the tutor from the class, or by leaving him to teach the class alone. Again, this would result in the substitution of an imitation model for the Double Focus approach.

Failure, too, by the tutor and teacher, together, to establish properly an agenda of learning for the students, so that they enter class without specific work to do, can lead to a distortion of the technique.

In other words, the entire process depends extensively on the establishing of very good relationships, and on shared understanding by tutor and teacher. This means making an investment of time and energy in establishing a sound basis for this work. But, of course, such relationships and understandings are fostered by the need to work together, and once established can be maintained with less effort.

The tutor's skill in negotiating with the school, and in communicating clearly the essentials of the technique, is also important. He must steer his way among potential ethical problems, and can be in difficulty if these are not properly understood by all the adults involved from the very beginning. The essence of the difficulties lies in the fine line between a genuinely open, enquiry-orientated attitude to what happens in class, and an offensively critical attitude by any of the adults. This could lead to a destructive/defensive vicious circle. (Although I am pleased to say this is not something that I have ever experienced, and it is certainly not a position that professional teachers readily adopt.)

Among other things, therefore, all parties must work towards a group responsibility for defining and maintaining professionalism. This too is an important part of the students' learning experiences. Broadly, an open approach is considerably helped by the teacher being present at the debriefing sessions, and being involved in the shaping of the students' programme of work. It is, for example, vital that teacher and tutor work together on devising any observation schedules or tasks.

A further limitation of this technique is that it offers help only with a fairly small (but significant) strand of the training course, and it copes only with some aspects of the teacher's role. Particularly, it does not deal with the vital area of discipline and control, except indirectly, because, since there are so many adults in the classroom, none of these issues arises. Further, it does not permit much 'solo' work for the student with the whole class, though it does require work with individuals and groups. But it does enable students to begin to recognise in themselves their own skills, dispositions, capacities, and knowledge, and to see how they begin to relate to the demands of the classroom. This technique might, therefore, be used intensively rather than extensively. And can offer significant help in laying the foundations for a professional life of teaching and learning to teach.

Its particular contributions

At a time when a student is newly orienting herself to the idea of being a teacher, the Double Focus technique can offer a great deal in breaking the closed circuit of her thinking – about knowledge, about learning, about herself, and about the process of becoming a teacher. And this breaking of the circuit is as important for graduates entering PGCE courses as it is for all those entering BEd courses.

Among some of the new demands on the student at the beginning of her course, are the following:

1. The need to be aware of the development of:
   — her own knowledge (of subjects, of pupils, of education)
   — her own attitudes to knowledge
   — traditional theories of knowledge.
2. The need to be aware of the new skills, abilities, and capacities which she, personally, must develop.
3. The need to be aware of her own attitudes, personality, capacities, and dispositions, particularly in respect of working with others with intent to enabling them to learn.

From among these complex areas, the Double Focus technique, working as one part of the students' programme, might be used to enable the student to recognise and begin to cope with the following:

1. Learning to split the mind: between one pupil and another, and between teacher's activities and pupils' tasks; between teaching and at the same time learning to teach; and between the immediate present and the future, so as to be prevenient for the pupils' welfare and learning. (This is particularly important where their previous academic work has required both the sixth-former and the graduate to learn to be single-minded.)
2. Taking on board the multiplicity of perspectives on the learning activities experienced in the normal classroom. The Double Focus technique copes well with this since it automatically draws on these and the additional level of the tutor's concerns, the tutor's concept of the students' concerns, and the actual concerns of the students.
3. Observing closely and thinking critically and analytically about practice.
4. Facing the problems of the complexity of relationships between theory and action, and learning to be a theorist, an experimenter, and a problem-solver. (As Sutton, 1975, p.338 says: 'continual testing of insights against experience is probably the core of a practical theory'.)
5. Learning what pupils (as distinct from siblings, friends, and adventure-

holiday or babysitting charges) are actually like, and what is involved in their learning across different ages and abilities.
6. Learning about herself, her own dispositions, capacities, values, and how they relate to her ability to work with other people. This includes issues like the exercising of imagination and judgement.
7. Understanding that teaching (enabling learning) is a cooperative enterprise.
8. Developing 'the understanding to monitor (her) own teaching, and the objectivity to carry out that task' (Hirst, 1976, p.18).
9. Contributing, herself, to this list, in the light of her own perceived needs, and in response to her own grappling with learning to learn to teach.

Such a list indicates aspects of teaching and learning which are deeper and more complex than any list of basic and advanced skills to be learnt. It is, by the same token, also more intellectually and personally demanding than such an approach, and therefore, perhaps, more calculated to motivate and challenge intending teachers and, importantly, to persuade them of the need to challenge and motivate their pupils.

This technique also offers considerable opportunities for eroding the barriers between teachers and tutors, schools and colleges, theory and practice. The extensive negotiations and preparations for this work are themselves a means of fostering better understanding both about the complex enterprise of training teachers and about the concomitant nature of teaching and learning to teach (and training and learning to train). Further, such partnership, unlike many government notions about the exchange of personnel, does not blur the roles of teacher and tutor, but gives each a properly respected place in the complex whole of preparing teachers for their work in schools.

The practical implications

The following is a tentative list of implications of working in this way.

For teachers

Teachers need to bring a range of skills and attitudes to this work. These include:

— a willingness, and an ability, to negotiate with the tutor about the philosophy and practicalities and to prepare with the tutor observation schedules and tasks
— understanding of the Double Focus teacher's role in the classroom
— a willingness to be seen as fallible, and to articulate worries in front of students
— the ability to accept, enjoy, and respond helpfully to critical analysis (as long as it is offered professionally)
— a willingness to see the need for and to share relevant information about

self and pupils
- willingness to become redundant in the classroom, briefly
- some knowledge of the rest of the students' course, including the reading and theoretical knowledge required of them
- an ability to remember what is known, felt, and needed by a new teacher (including editing out comments which are prejudicial to student preparation – like 'I never prepare lessons' or 'It's a doddle isn't it?')
- experience in self-appraisal
- an ability to see beyond the 'immersion model' and to realise that students should not be involved with pupils all of the classroom time, but need to be allowed to detach themselves from the proceedings
- respect for and understanding of the role of the tutor
- an ability to discriminate between what a student can do, and what an experienced teacher can
- a thorough understanding that the aim is not to produce 'clones' of either teacher or tutor
- some basic knowledge about classroom observation and observation techniques.

The following are the areas in which teachers might gain as a result of this work:

- new perspectives on their own work
- a sharpening up of their own self-appraisal, and increased knowledge of classroom observation techniques
- knowledge of up-to-the-minute information about current teacher training
- additional help in the classroom
- enjoyment of working with a group of adults who are usually very quick to see the point of the work, and are usually genuinely appreciative of it.

The following are requirements that teachers will need to make of others:

- time: to meet and prepare with the tutor
    to meet tutor and students for debriefing
    to prepare the class
- a reasonable sized room in which to work with 17 extra adults
- opportunity to meet students and tutor in college as well as school
- knowledge about the students as individuals
- an understanding that we are all human and that we can all learn from failures and the unintentional as well as, or even better than, the perfectly executed plan.

For tutors

The following are required from tutors as part of this work:

- a real grasp of the technique and its requirements
- skill in communicating this and in negotiating with the school and the

teacher
- respect for and understanding of the role of the teacher
- the ability to establish a mutually worthwhile programme with the teacher
- the need to maintain professionalism among all parties
- knowledge of and the ability to use observation techniques and tasks, and where necessary, the tact and ability to initiate the teacher in these things
- the ability to plan and execute a complicated programme which brings theory and practice into meaningful relationship
- the ability to think fast on his feet in the classroom and to harness all that happens into meaningful learning for the students
- the ability to establish an atmosphere in which real questions can be asked and real reactions can be safely shared, and where the teacher as well as the students can agonise openly about problematic issues
- the ability to keep the situation open so that students can achieve their own learning, and are not constrained by one uncongenial interpretation of events or motives.

The following are what might be gained by the tutor:

- new things to learn, about teaching and learning on every occasion
- a sense that his skills, of the planning, negotiating, managing, and enabling reflection, both during the lesson and after it, are met and matched by the teacher's technical skills in working with his pupils and talking about this (ie, a genuine sense of partnership where each partner has his own proper role and self-respect as well as the respect of the other)
- a sense that students' learning has progressed.

The tutor/teacher might reasonably demand from others:

- the opportunity to try out this way of working without prejudice, before it is dismissed out of hand
- the resources of time and cooperation from teacher/tutor, students, schools, and importantly, his own institution.

For students

The following is a list of what might be required of them:

- commitment to learning and willingness to engage in this at an intellectual level as well as a practical one
- cooperation with teacher and tutor, even when what is happening has not been revealed beforehand
- ability to work with pupils and adults
- ability to split the mind
- willingness to reflect, and to learn from this
- ability to observe in detail
- the motivation to use what is offered and to shape it to her own learning

— toleration of what might be seen as a twilight zone in which the student is neither a student alone, but is not yet quite a solo teacher.

As a result, the student might be expected to gain insight into teaching and how to enable learning, which should be of use in preparing, executing, and reflecting upon her own practical work.

Part 3

Sustained School Experience: Some Changes in Practice

11. Partners in Crime: Theory Mislaid

Summary

- The preparation for teaching practice
  — the college's role
  — whose responsibilities?
  — the school's role
- The class teacher's role during practice
  — why it is central
  — some conflicting demands
  — some models of class teachers' attitudes to TP supervision
  — their underlying assumptions
- The tutor's role during practice
  — tutor as reactive to the teacher
  — some dilemmas
  — the assumptions underlying the tutor's role
- The student's role during practice
  — some dilemmas
- Teachers and tutors as partners in crime
  — the crimes

Introduction

The intention of this chapter is to fuel discussion about how teachers might learn professional practice by offering a critique of that ordinary kind of TP which has been traditional of teacher-training institutions since at least the second world war, and which still prevails today. By ordinary TP is meant the normal school placement for a block period which is provided by the school and overseen or supervised by an assigned college tutor who makes a regular visit to the school. Though the term 'sustained school experience' is now accorded to this activity, the original term TP is used here to denote the traditional aspect of what is being described.

Basically, the assumptions at work in traditional TP have been that learning to teach is a simple process of working in an apprentice relationship to an experienced teacher with a college tutor as an overseer with an oilcan. In this traditional model, therefore, the relationships between teacher and tutor are based on the assumption that each has his own separate role in the TP: the teacher with a priority for the best interests of the class, the tutor as overseer of the student's *performance*, and both leaving the student to *learn* from the practice by some unidentified form of osmosis.

The preparation for teaching practice

Although it is often given scant attention by either college or school because of the pressure of other priorities, the very way in which the practice is prepared for by both institutions is of major significance. The omissions often still include: the failure of school and college together to establish a joint understanding of the place of the practice in the whole course; and the failure to elucidate the intentions and the focus of the activities of the TP for teacher, tutor, and student. This has also meant a resultant inattention to the respective roles of teacher and tutor during the practice.

All of this is best demonstrated by looking in detail at the role of the college and school during the preparatory period.

The college's role

Many colleges have viewed the setting up of TP as a matter of simple administration involving only the actual placement of the student. This is now called into question by the facts that:

— the training course itself is now conceived differently
— TP now plays a very different role in the student's learning to teach
— a partnership in training is now supposed to exist.

Clearly, it is the joint partners' responsibility to agree, at the micro level, the intentions of the practice, the roles of the partners in it, and the detailed focus of the student's work. But this needs to be done within a proper framework. It must be the college's responsibility to initiate the liaison with the school, to explain the context of the practice and its role in the student's overall course and to prepare the student for the work in school.

Whose responsibilities?

However, there are grey areas about how far the college's sole responsibility goes. They have always been grey, and the advent of partnership has not (in most cases) served to clarify them. For example, in the preparation of *students* for practice, how much information should the college require students to obtain during the pre-practice visit? How far should the college lay down requirements for such visits? Who should vet students' paperwork? How should they be assessed, and by whom? Tradition has made most of this the tutor's concern, guided by instinct and experience. CATE regulations now shift it to the shoulders of teachers, with no additional guidance.

The class teacher is said by some to be the most powerful figure of the TP in terms of influence upon the student. Yet there are so many things that the class teacher often does not know about the practice, most of which need to be understood before it begins. For example, he often does not know about:

— the course the student is on
— the reasons for the student's particular requirements during practice
— what his own role is supposed to be
— how the assessment is to be carried out and why
— what kind of attitude to theory the college, the tutor, and the student take
— what the procedures of the practice should be
— how students are expected to *learn* from the practice
— what role in this learning the teacher is supposed to have
— what links he is supposed to have with the college
— what are the college's expectations of the school
— with whom to communicate, and how, if things go wrong.

Responsibility for these issues ought now to be jointly held if partnership means anything.

The school's role

There are, however, further responsibilities which the school alone, and particularly the head or a senior deputy, must shoulder, and which again often receive scant consideration. These are:

— the reasons for placing a student with staff (How often is it really because that member of staff is particularly good at helping the student to *theorise* about (reflect upon) her practice?)
— the preparation of the staff for the pre-practice visit (How often: is the timetable available in all its details before the practice? are the lessons sorted out? are the resources available? is the teacher talked through what will be expected of him? is the class prepared in all points for the student to take over?)
— the reasons for placing the *class* with the student (How often across their primary and secondary schooling do some pupils have students?)
— do schools have a proper routine for organising and monitoring these things?

Preparation, then, is not, in the traditional model of TP, guided by theoretical considerations, despite the tremendous amount of practice from which such theory might have been exhumed. The same is true of the teacher's role.

The class teacher's role during practice

Why it is central

Among the kaleidoscope of variables which are inevitably brought to the experience of TP, and which can so crucially affect the student and the assessment of her performance, the one which is perhaps most vital and which both the tutor and the student seem to feel they have least control over is the influence of the class teacher's view of TP. Curiously, the teacher's role in and attitude to TP have received relatively little attention from heads (or whoever places the student within the school), from teacher trainers, or from researchers. Yet how the teacher sees TP (both in general and in the particular) has a profound effect upon the process and progress of the practice. Indeed, compared with many of the variables in the TP which either the tutor or the student can influence directly (like pupils' attitudes, the classroom environment or teaching styles and materials), the basic attitude of the teacher towards TP itself is unlikely to be altered easily. It becomes the baseline from which the rest follows, and is a key to the success or failure of the practice. It not only may affect the actual assigned or assessed level of success of the student on the practice, but (in some ways more importantly) it can also affect *the scope for learning* of the student.

For example, a class teacher might see the demands of TP *either* as something to be got through by student, teacher, and class, with minimum disruption to the class, *or* as something simply requiring the provision of a good teacher-model, to be watched and then copied by the student. Either of these is inevitably liable (consciously or not) to restrict the student's scope for creativity, for reflection on her own preferred methods, for learning about herself, for making mistakes and taking chances, by shutting the student into a narrow range of possibilities and a narrow view of teaching. Ironically, these approaches are often chosen with the very best intentions.

Some conflicting demands

TP often serves to heighten the class teacher's awareness of a number of conflicting demands. Particularly irksome can be those stemming from the desire and need always to improve the lot of the pupils and their learning in the face of, or in direct conflict to, the concerns of the student and her learning. Thus, the teacher daily during the practice has to resolve a number of practical dilemmas related to the best deployment of his and the student's time, energy, and focus. He has to decide, for example:

— when to teach himself, or to let the student do so
— whether to 'give' (or allow) the student a favourite and showy topic and risk it not being done so well or exploited so fully as he himself would do it, or to encourage a duller but safer subject and method
— whether to give over the class now or to hang on to them for just one more hour and leave the student to make the best of watching, so that the pupils will 'profit more'
— whether his time is best spent in class watching the student closely and working with her, or working at the back of the class, or outside it on resources for his own later use with that class
— whether to allow the student scope to try something her own way with its concomitant risks and rewards, or to restrict that ambition for what might *(or might not be)* the greater good of the pupils.

Such (common) dilemmas are understandable, arise from the best of motives, and are certainly not easily diverted by the student or the tutor's intervention. Yet when teachers are brought to look at them closely and coldly they can be seen to be based on false assumptions which revolve around false distinction about what is best for pupils and student, and misunderstandings about how students learn. They also spring from failure to grasp the role of the class teacher in supervision, and the role of risk-taking, mistakes, and reflection in experiential learning.

The following provocative model has been constructed as a means of pursuing the logic of these attitudes. It typifies attitudes to, and views of, TP. While it is merely as crude a representation of a complex human activity as any other model, it provides a means of considering a spectrum of approaches, from the least to the most concerned about the class and, conversely, from the most to the least helpful in terms of students' (or pupils') learning.

Some models of class teachers' attitudes to TP supervision

1. The Total Immersion or Sink-or-Swim model

This sees the teacher as willing to let the class try the student out, and denotes a detachment about the end result. Here the teacher has no real role in helping the student to learn and is even detached from the short-term progress of the pupils. Here it is the pupils who are the key means of teaching the student – if the student has the ability to listen and to watch them. Rumour suggests that this attitude is now unfashionable, but it often lurks under staffroom conversations.

2. The Watch Me and Copy model

This sees the student's key way of learning to teach as modelling a master. It is caught in phrases like: 'Just do what I do dear', or 'See – it's easy really, isn't it?', or 'She needs to go back and watch (copy) some good teachers'. This model has no developed ideas about supervisory activities, or about how the student learns, but simply looks for conformity in the student to that particular teacher's accepted methods.

3. The Spare Pair of Hands model

This model is beloved of beleaguered teachers who are seeking to do the best for their class by spreading themselves as far as possible among them, and who cannot see beyond this. It assumes that the student will learn by working beside the teacher, but it neglects the following vital issues for the student:

— the need to take responsibility for the whole class, not just a few fill-in tasks
— the need to find her own way of doing things, not to conform to someone else's
— the need to learn from and during the experience via reflection
— the need to make her own mistakes on her own, as a major means of

learning.

This model thus sees the teacher as abdicating all supervisory responsibilities outside the lesson itself, and losing the value of learning by working together.

4. The Playing Safe model

Here the teacher's only concern is for the class and for the continuation of the teacher's methods and techniques as well as the topic. The student has everything done for her except the teaching itself. The assumption is that as well as protecting the class, this approach is a help and great support to the student. As such is also assumes that no further supervision is necessary since all risks and potential dangers have been prestructured out of the proceedings by the teacher's own good organisation, *before* the student takes the lesson. This, of course, ignores the human aspects of teaching and the student's own preferred modes of operation, and often results in the frustrating experience that in spite of (because of) all that had been done for the student, the lesson is a failure.

5. The Unwilling Sacrifice model

This is a version of the Playing Safe model. It assumes that the class as well as the teacher would really rather continue as usual and not sacrifice time to students' learning. It results in the class teacher's refusal to give up the class *this* week. Like model 4, it assumes that the only responsibility the teacher has is for the class, that the student will learn just as much, if not more, by watching, since TP is a time-consuming evil which is best reduced whenever possible.

6. The Subversive Defender model

The attitude enshrined here is one which is overprotective to the student and automatically unsympathetic or even antagonistic to the supervisor. It is prevalent in teachers with mother-hen attitudes to pupils and students and in those with anti-authority attitudes. Very often the kind of conspiracy of silence between teacher and (not always entirely willing) student actually becomes more of a priority than does reflecting on and learning from the lesson.

7. The Self-Comparison model

This model leads the teacher to compare the student's performance to a half-remembered and no longer relevant vision of what that teacher himself was like during TP, and thus to treat oversympathetically the student's failures, which, with stronger handling, might have been better harnessed to the student's real learning. The supervision resulting from this romantic and self-deceiving attitude is often valueless in terms of the student's progress in learning to teach.

8. The Attacker/Defender model

This is an opposite version of that found in model 6. The attitude to the student and the supervision is that it must reach for the ideal, *and* that technical mastery *is* attainable. Accordingly, the teacher's activities are dedicated to proving either that the student has or has not mastered teaching. This is a model which results from the Competency-based Learning approach discussed in Chapter 5.

9. The Pincer Model or Strategic Partnership model

The first of three partnership models, this assumes that the teacher and tutor will work together to help improve the student, and that this is best done by each tackling the same aspects of the student's learning. The choice of aspect is usually made by the teacher. One of the partners then adopts the tough approach while the other assumes a gentler one. Supervision is still, ironically, on the whole pursued separately and in a narrowly focused way, in spite of these strategic decisions.

10. The Pragmatic Appraisal Partnership model

Here the teacher works with the tutor and both work pragmatically in dealing with the student. The basis of the work is appraisal by both teacher and tutor of the student's performance. The student's ability to learn is considered as part of this, but the roles of teacher and tutor as facilitators of the student's learning are given a very narrow interpretation. That is, the only way the student is expected to learn is via the teacher's and tutor's critical comments. Among other things this model therefore does not foster the student's own autonomy as a reflective practitioner.

11. The Collaborative Minders model

Here the teacher is willing to divide up with the tutor the areas of the student's work to be concentrated upon. Thus, each takes responsibility for a different aspect of the supervision, but neither considers the whole of it. Further, the notion of supervision is more that of a minder than of a facilitating supervisor. The tendency here is for the class teacher to look after (mind) the class and to raise with the student only those matters which affect its welfare, while the tutor deals with (minds) the process of assessment of the student's performance across a number of sample lessons.

12. The Abdication model

This is, as it sounds, a model in which the class teacher or tutor claims pressure of work elsewhere and takes no responsibility at all for the standard or quality of the student's work with classes or her own learning from that work. This attitude, alas, is more common than might be supposed, or is admitted.

13. The Neutral Sympathiser model

This model tends to appear at the point or internal or external examination of

TP. Here the teacher is happy for the tutor to make a decision, particularly an adverse decision about the student's performance, but prefers to take a sympathetic line with the student – without, of course, actually contradicting the tutor's decision.

14. The Double Standards model
This model is often adopted by class teachers and the more senior staff in schools where a student is near to failing the final practice. The attitude is best summed up in one version of the words often heard at this point. 'Well of course *we* wouldn't employ her because she needs more support than we have time to offer next year, but perhaps someone else will be willing to support her until she finds her feet. After all, who knows, she might be all right with more practice.'

Their underlying assumptions

The above models are *all* drawn from the apprenticeship view of initial training, with its assumptions about learning to teach and how to facilitate it. A look at these assumptions shows why these ways of operating are now considered by some as a crime. The following points may be made:

1. Enabling a student to learn to teach is assumed to involve only:

— providing a reasonable practical placement
— providing the opportunities for practice
— providing the opportunities for watching, copying, and/or working alongside a master model
— offering a critical appraisal based on concern for the class being taught but no real awareness or understanding of the student's learning needs
— encouraging self-appraisal by means of first offering a lesson criticism
— expecting the student to be able to reflect upon her teaching in order to improve the situation for the class, without offering examples of the complex processes of such self-reflection in practice
— assuming that the way the teacher works is what the student should seek to approximate to
— assuming that means and ends issues and the moral dimension of the lesson content and the teaching methods are neither open to discussion nor need to be (in other words, that traditional topics and methods have always been acceptable and that the student should start from these without questioning their educational ends)
— believing that plenty of practice following 'the right kind of model' is all that is required to improve practice for all those except the natural failures.

2. The role of the teacher during the student's TP is seen:

— as avoiding being a supervisor, since this would be abrogating the tutor's role
— as at best establishing a partnership with the tutor in appraisal of the student as performer, at worst as establishing no relationship whatever,

and generally walking carefully round the tutor
- as guardian of the interests of the class, not as an enabler of the student's learning (except as a means of safeguarding the class)
- as polite host to the visiting tutor with a view to protecting the image of the class and school
- as witness to, but not a party to, the assessment of the student
- as a successful practitioner who knows what to do, but does not expect to have to (claims he never has time to) articulate even to himself a detailed rationale for the principles and procedures he adopts
- as an expert in all matters related to his own classroom, but who does not expect to have to articulate that expertise in detail
- as one who sees expert knowledge as absolutist rather than temporary and who is not accustomed to being challenged about his knowledge, even by his own thinking
- as a professional who deals in immediate practical decisions and thus must reduce (or ignore) the complexity and problematic nature of educational issues, and who encourages the student to do the same
- as naturally and acceptably unaware of the detail of the student's course of training as a whole, and therefore as assuming that all that matters on TP is the student's successful performance and the safety of the class
- as a practitioner who has considerable doubts about Educational Theory and who seeks in contrast to concentrate on the student's practical expertise, often by simply *telling* the student what he thinks of her work
- as a critic of the student's performance, who adopts a transmission mode in teaching the student while wanting the student to teach by means of problem-solving in the classroom.

This rather crude and reductionist approach to the description of the teacher's role is offered merely as a challenge to the class teacher and tutor to consider these matters. And there is certainly no implication in it that the tutor's role in the model is any less a crime than the teacher's. Indeed, he should be held *largely responsible* for it, as is indicated below.

The tutor's role during practice

Tutor as reactive to the teacher

As has already been implied above, the tutor can allow the teacher's attitudes to TP to manoeuvre him into a reactive role. This is often excused by acute awareness that he is a guest in the school and the classroom, and that without the cooperation of both school and class teacher, there would be no TP. Until the tutor is willing or able to be more articulate about his own role, and negotiates roles with the teacher and the student in the light of the intentions of the practice and the place of the practice in the whole course, these problems will continue.

It is for these reasons that the tutor's role can still be seen as balancing or acting as foil to the teacher-roles described above. In all cases, then, he is the assessor of the student's performance – an examiner first and a supervisor second. And this forces the lesson critique to be given to rather than elicited from the student.

Some dilemmas

Part of the reason for all of this is that the supervising tutor, like the teacher, is subject to a number of practical dilemmas – in this case about the TP enterprise. Most of these stem from the following:

— his position as guest in the school
— his position, in the eyes of the class teacher, as useless theorist rather than practitioner
— the pressures from schools and government for him to conform to their view that he *should* be an expert in practice when in fact the most useful thing he can offer is a deeper understanding of theory and practice, and of how students learn through practice
— the expectation of teacher and student that he should supply, rapidly, ready solutions to all the practical problems met by the student, when in fact he is trying to get the student to offer solutions and to understand that these are problematic and temporary and need to be endlessly reconsidered
— the fact that even to try to explain the above issues to the class teacher is a risky business since it probably challenges some of his most deeply held convictions
— the eternal pressures of time which preclude teacher and tutor from discussing issues in depth and the need to spend what time is available with the *student*
— the problem of trying to register, in opposition to other priorities, the urgent need for such discussion in the light of the changing nature of TP and its role in the course.

The assumptions underlying the tutor's role

Thus, from the tutor's point of view, his reactive role contains the following assumptions:

1. He alone is a supervisor and an assessor, and should not expect the teacher to do his job – especially the less pleasant aspects of it.
2. He is an appraiser of the student's performance across a small sample of lessons in the classroom, and can have no generally established process for learning about and taking account of all the aspects of the student's work that he does not see.
3. He is there, pursuing a transmission model, to *inform* the student of how *he* sees her progress, and therefore merely to *react to* what she does rather than to work on a problem-solving basis *with* her as she proceeds.
4. He is a safeguarder of the college's reputation and assessment

procedures.
5. As a guest in the school he should not raise issues which might be contentious in the short term, but should preserve the school-college relationship and the associated TP places in the long term.
6. He is one who can talk about practice, but is incapable of actually doing it in today's conditions.
7. He is an expert in formal theory but this is irrelevant to the student's practice.
8. He is more concerned to give weight to the problematic nature of the educational issues involved in the practice than to respond to the demands of the practical situation.
9. He is the only one who could (should?) make any links between the TP and the rest of the student's course (he is the only one who believes that there is any relevance in the rest of the student's course).

The crime central to this approach to TP is that the student's learning through practice slips through the gap between the teacher's prime concern with the class and the tutor's concern with performance, procedures, and with playing the diplomat.

The student's role during practice

Some dilemmas

The student's position between the class teacher (host) and visiting tutor-appraiser is certainly not an easy one. Her dilemmas may arise from the following problems:

1. She is caught between the need to please and respond to the teacher whose class she has and who therefore must be kept happy daily, and to impress and please the tutor whose assessment will be what counts at the end of the practice but who only samples her work in performance weekly.
2. She is caught between a view that learning to teach merely involves copying (conforming to) a good teacher-model together with repeated practice (which automatically will make near-perfect), and the requirements of her college, which via her file lead her to plan ahead and to write an appraisal of (reflect upon) her work.
3. She is caught between a sense that there is far more to teaching than appears on the surface, and the fact that her final mark can depend superficially on her performance, and on her abilities in what is known as 'impression management'.
4. She is encouraged to use problem-solving and experiential learning techniques with pupils, thus beginning to see herself in a supportive role as an enabler of learning, and yet in her own learning she finds both teachers and tutors adopting methods more consistent with traditional transmission methods in which she is told about (given an appraisal of)

her own experiences!
5. She is taught at college, and encouraged in the school, to consider that her role as a teacher is far wider than that of 'classroom teacher', and yet the assessment of her practice is invariably made on the basis of how she performs in a few specific class lessons.
6. She can be seen by a tutor teaching all of her best (or worst) sessions, and can be convinced that a distorted view of her performance has been gained. If she discusses this with an adamant tutor or a sympathetic, but powerless teacher, she may get nowhere.

Teachers and tutors as partners in crime

Arguably, then, this vicious circle, with its implications of unconscious sin on the part of the class teacher and errors of omission on the part of the tutor, constitutes a crime.

The first step to breaking such a circle (which has already been breached in many parts of the country) is to face the real nature of the crimes.

The crimes

They are all crimes of omission. The following is an attempt to summarise the most important. They are the failure of these partners:

— to see the need to facilitate the student's own *learning* from practice and to understand and take account of what that learning involves and what this implies for both teachers and tutors

— to link the kinds of problem-solving activities now used to facilitate the learning from practice by *pupils* with approaches to the student's own learning from practice, and to conceive the TP as a series of problem-solving activities

— to relinquish outdated views, assumptions, and attitudes about each other, and about theory and practice

— to ensure the survival of theory instead of allowing the development of a theory of survival

— to face together, discuss, and ultimately to find agreement on how to foster the student's development of personal theories of teaching which can be exhumed from action, as well as helping her to draw usefully on formal theory

— to be able clearly to articulate their own theories of action and to develop a common mode of discourse, both in respect of TP supervision and in respect of their own teaching, and thus their inability to provide real examples in their own work of the kind of reflection and deliberation they expect of the student

— to tackle TOGETHER the building of a partnership which acknowledges BOTH areas of difference AND areas of agreement over the following aspects of the teacher's and tutor's professional approach:

preparation for and the intentions of the practice; the place of the TP within the whole course; their expertise; knowledge; beliefs; values; concerns; views; expectations and roles

— to recognise that the quality of the *pupils'* learning and the quality of the *student's* learning from practice are inextricably interlinked and can become areas of joint concern, joint priority, and joint improvement
— to see that time and effort which is set aside to seek beneath the surface of practice and to articulate and help the student articulate the rationale for her work, is as vital a preparation for the next lesson as writing the next lesson plan or marking pupils' work
— to carry out together a full evaluation of the TP to discover what *they* learnt in addition to what the student has.

But such failure also indicates the way forward. Many courses are no longer organised on the assumption that theory and practice are totally separate. If, in the course structure, practice is now interwoven sequentially with theory, if the goal is now a reflective practitioner, and if the development of a personal theory from practice is a key activity in learning to teach, then the *entire role* of TP within the course and within the student's learning programme needs to be reconceptualised.

That this reconceptualisation has not always taken place among college and school partners in training even when course design has changed, is the contention of this chapter.

In the light of these, let us now turn to a rather different way of organising sustained school experience.

12. A Deliberative Approach: Relocating Practice, or Refocusing Training?

Summary

- Refocusing the entire enterprise
  - a possible goal for professional practice
  - resultant problems for initial training
  - the implications of these
  - relocating teacher training
- Reconsidering supervision
  - the nature of supervision
  - supervision as a discrete expertise
- Issues in assessment
  - the purpose of assessment
  - traditional criteria for assessment
  - new approaches to assessment
- Deliberative supervision
  - rediscovering theory
  - recasting supervision
  - reshaping the post-lesson conference

Introduction

Sustained school experience becomes a totally different activity from traditional TP when it is located in the reflective practitioner view of professional training, and when the procedures of the course revolve around investigation, reflection, and deliberation. What might be called a deliberative approach to the supervision of sustained experience might then be adopted. Such a deliberative approach might also be usefully used within the structure set up to support licensed teachers working in school towards QTS. But such changes of intention and procedure in supervision and assessment, and those resulting from new provisions for licensed teachers, are not without their own demands, as this chapter demonstrates. However the training of teachers proceeds in future, arguably it must be based upon an attempt to come to grips with the heart of the problem of how to enable trainees to learn through practice. For this reason, refocusing the training is far more important, educationally, than relocating it in schools.

Refocusing the entire enterprise

Part of the problem of traditional TP is that it neither grapples with nor works towards a view of what society demands from professionals, or of what professional practice demands from its exponents. Yet the goal of producing a reflective practitioner derives from a consideration of these, and is in no way diminished, but rather is made more urgent, by the new demands of the 1988 Education Reform Act.

A possible goal for professional practice

As indicated in Chapter 1 the world of professional practice is, in every field today, a fast-moving one. Continuous developments in and discoveries about knowledge and understanding can daily affect the whole range of the professional practitioner's expertise. The trainee can be more up-to-date than her qualified counterpart. More than ever, clients are given, and expect to be made privy to, information and explanation which previously was of a professionally privileged nature. Clearly, then, any goal for professional training must take account of these things and allow for the continuous revision which the above influences now demand. Particularly, perhaps, it should take account of the practitioner's need to:

— exercise with responsibility relevant skills, knowledge, abilities, dispositions, capacities, and understanding
— be able continuously to uncover and create his own theories of action and to use and evaluate these
— be able to work with people in order to facilitate their best interests in terms of learning
— concomitantly and continuously to be able to adapt and refine all these things.

Given all this, the following might be (in many cases already is) a valid general ideal for the qualified practitioner:

To possess the skills, ability, dispositions, understanding, and capacity continuously to create, discover, use, and evaluate his own theories of action in order that in all his work with his pupils he is committed to facilitating their learning to their highest potential, and concomitantly *to learning himself how better to do so.*

This must not, of course, be taken to imply that no further in-service training will be needed for such professionals as attain this state. The reverse is true, since this kind of enquiry-oriented approach to professional practice needs a range of additional support and needs to be embedded in a wider and widening context of professional understanding and knowledge.

Resultant problems for initial training

The problems which arise from the professional practitioner's goal as stated above stem from our (as yet) lack of adequate knowledge of and exploration of the following:

1. how to go about developing in the trainee either the ability or the capacity continuously to create, discover, and evaluate her own theories of action
2. how to help her use and translate a range of useful kinds of theory, so that theory enlightens practice and practice theory, and intuition and instinct are turned into insight
3. how to cultivate in the trainee the disposition to approach her professional duties in these ways
4. how to assess these capacities, dispositions, and abilities (or even how to be sure of recognising them) on a short-term training course
5. how a trainee actually learns from practice, and how (whether) such learning affects future practice
6. which aspects of theory are most helpful to the trainee in order to achieve these goals
7. how to reach consensus about the most important characteristics of the professional practitioner's role
8. how, during sustained school experience, the qualified professional on the placement (teacher) and the trainer (tutor) should divide up the role of supervision, or how the licensed teacher should be supported.

The implications of these

Professional pre-service and in-service training operate in an essentially problematic context, and by many uncharted means. From this apparently very negative position, it might be argued that several positive possibilities arise.

First, if all of those involved admit the problematic nature and many little-understood aspects of professional training, it might provide a clearer, more secure, and *common* basis from which to begin the work of understanding better and thus improving the processes of training.

Second, in our very admission of this we might face squarely the probable significance for trainee and trainers of focusing deliberately on the problematic, the unsuccessful, and the unknown as a real means of advancing our knowledge, rather than brushing them under the carpet in favour of the safe but simplistic and ultimately useless notions of teaching, learning, and professional practice which currently often prevail in discussions.

Relocating teacher training

Whether or not future training is based exclusively in the schools, the key issue in the preparation of teachers is how to turn it from a process of initiation into old traditions of working and consequent reinforcement of conservative notions of teaching and learning (apprenticeship model) to a process of investigation and exploration (research model). The central shift, then, is not of physical location but of reconceptualisation. What is being argued here is that the enterprise of learning to teach should be relocated within the ambit of curriculum studies and research, and thus refocused. This would mean that by comparison with traditional TP (which simplifies processes), all of the activities of learning to teach would be treated as curriculum problems – that is, as uncertain problems for which any practical solutions will be regarded as temporary. (See Reid, 1978, pp.46–50.)

Thus, the substantive issues of teacher training, even from the beginning, are not merely concerned with technical know-how about teaching or the investigation of it, but focus on how to make better decisions about what should be taught and about methods. Thus, the moral dimensions of teaching decisions are brought more into the centre of consciousness, and the entire enterprise becomes deliberative. For this to occur, the trainee will need help from supervisors, no matter how the basic training is organised.

If this approach is taken seriously, arguably, the trainee not only learns in a more realistic way what it is like to do a job where there are few easy solutions and where new decisions have to be taken daily, but she also sees those with whom she is training applying to their own work the same techniques which they require of her. In other words, she sees her supervisors, in *their* professional work of training her, adhering to the goal of attempting continuously to create, use and evaluate their own theories of action in order that they facilitate her learning (to her highest and best potential), and concomitantly attempting to learn how better to do so.

Thus, the challenge of trying, temporarily, to resolve the problematic is shared by trainers and qualified professionals with the students themselves in training *as a part of that training*. This reconceptualisation has major implications for supervision and assessment, which will not be removed by relocating training in the schools.

Reconsidering supervision

The nature of supervision

The apprenticeship or traditional model of TP as discussed in Chapter 11, essentially sees the student as a passive agent who is manipulated into producing a good live performance, and views the nature of supervision as preparing for, witnessing, and offering a critique of a rehearsal with a live audience.

Yet, the newer models of clinical and counselling supervision (of, say, Stones, 1984, and Smyth, 1986) or even of coaching of Schön (1987b) are little better in this respect. Here the nature of supervision is that of expert working with client to shape and discuss the issues leading to or arising from practice. The supervisor is still an expert in the practice, though he has now added to that expertise an ability to work in a counselling mode (which is also rapidly becoming a normal aspect of teaching). Indeed, one of the indirect results of this newer approach is that it can settle the student-supervisor relationship back into a pupil-teacher relationship.

The nature of TP supervision, then, is that most models have not broken out of the notion that the student-supervisor relationship is the same as, though one level up from, the pupil-teacher one.

With the deliberative approach to TP, supervisors (teacher and tutor) become partners with the student in enquiry into the practice of teaching and supervision. Here there are no experts in teaching and learning, and so collaborative enquiry, reflection, and deliberation become the key activities. But such collaboration should not obscure the different and complementary abilities and knowledge brought by each. It does, however, behove all the partners to understand the distinct nature of supervision.

Supervision as a discrete expertise

The question remains, then, what *is* involved in being a good supervisor? Wherein lies the supervisor's expertise? The following points are clearly central (see also Cameron-Jones, 1987):

1. Facilitating good practice in others is different from being a good practitioner. Indeed, it should not surprise us if some good practitioners do not even want to be involved in facilitating the practical learning of those in training.
2. Facilitating good practice in others means helping *them* to learn from their own experience.
3. It involves familiarity with and understanding of the kinds of classroom situation in which the student is working, but does not necessarily mean having taught successfully or otherwise either that class or a similar one.
4. Good supervision is improved by having access to information about the class and the teaching context from one who is intimate with it. However, the danger here is that the teacher, who has taken the class, who will return to it, and who may be protective of it, is not necessarily the best supervisor of the student, since he could be tempted to prevent the very kinds of risk-taking which would facilitate the student's learning.
5. Good supervision involves helping students to investigate and to reflect upon and deliberate about what they are doing, are trying to do, or are failing to do. These activities go well beyond the realms of questions about which technical skill could have been used at a particular moment in the classroom. They promote consideration of the moral aspects of the student's intentions (the ends as well as the means).
6. Helping students in this way involves the supervisor in enabling *them* to reflect upon practice, to draw theory out of practice and to bring relevant formal theory up to practice. The supervisor must, therefore, be familiar with the common mode of discourse of this education approach (including the language of theory), with a variety of investigation and evaluation techniques for use in the classroom and the school, and their possible use and limitations in enabling the student to learn from practice.
7. Helping a student to be able to do these things involves the supervisor in being able to work alongside the student in helping her to learn from

mistakes as well as successes, by enabling her, by means of practical reasoning (deliberation), to draw out from these the lessons to be learnt at the level of principles rather than practical tips.
8. This involves a relationship with the student in which both are genuinely learning to learn, by means of a problem-solving approach, and in which the supervisor is an expert in:
   (a) working with students at practical problem-solving in the classroom and how to draw upon a range of approaches
   (b) the workings of the individual class, the background of the pupils, and how they operate within the context of the whole school and other lessons.

These responsibilities might easily be divided between a teacher and a tutor, not arbitrarily but according to what each brings.

Issues in assessment

The reconceptualisation of learning to teach, and the possible relocation of the process, as described above, raise a number of issues about the purposes of, and the criteria for, the assessment of sustained school experience.

The purpose of assessment

In the traditional model of TP, the assessment of the student's practical competence has, almost exclusively, an administrative rather than an educational role in the training course.

The first assessment is usually diagnostic and intended to alert students and staff to those who are unsuitable for the profession; this, or a later one, becomes the basis of the student's reference, and the final practice is a means of gaining entry to the profession via QTS. And it seems reasonable to suggest that assessment of practice will have to continue to act as a gateway to professional practice whatever the form of training (though from time to time this has been questioned, see Stones, 1984). But whatever is provided in the way of written criteria for tutors and teachers, and whoever will judge the progression towards QTS, almost everything about assessment inevitably remains problematic.

In the traditional model, then, the educational purpose of assessment is often obscured by these formal aspects. However, when training takes on the nature described above, the purposes of assessment are also affected, and the focus of assessment is changed. Here, the student's contribution becomes part of the process, and assessment becomes a means of learning for real the important and necessary professional skills of appraisal, and of coming to see their problematic nature, both in terms of the criteria for assessment, and in terms of their performance-based nature.

In order to see the extent of change in assessment that this involves it is necessary to look briefly at the kind of criteria proposed for traditional courses.

Traditional criteria for assessment

As was discussed in Chapter 6, many of the central decisions and judgements made during professional training about both the training and the student's teaching rest upon crucial distinctions about whether teaching is essentially seen as an art or a science. The apprenticeship model of TP assumes that teaching is essentially a scientific (logical-rational) activity. In course design on the traditional product model, this usually means that considerable numbers of criteria are captured on paper and deemed measurable or at least observable. But there are in reality deep disagreements about what these criteria are, which are priority areas, whether it is present achievements or future potential that is being assessed, and how such assessment should be recorded. Examples of schedules of criteria for assessment abound. Yet when these are examined in detail they usually reveal a number of interesting points.

For example:

— they usually concentrate on performance of observable teaching skills and refer less frequently to pupils' learning
— they are rarely geared to take account of the unpredictable happenings in the classroom
— they often ignore the complexity of the teacher's task and rarely focus upon the holistic view
— they omit the full range of perspectives on the student's work, including the student's.

In other words they take a rational managerial or scientific view of teaching, mainly because these aspects are easier to identify both theoretically as characteristics of teaching, and in practice in classroom observation.

By contrast, what is needed in the reflective practitioner model is a system which:

— offers a means of monitoring the trainee's ongoing *processes* of learning
— requires the trainee to take part in the assessment procedure itself
— copes with aspects like the continuous adaptation and refinement of practice, and the ability to reflect upon it, deliberate about it, and investigate it.

What, then, are the implications of this?

New approaches to assessment

As Cameron-Jones usefully points out, both teacher (or, perhaps, QTS assessor) and student need to be clear and in agreement about what the student is to be assessed on, about the evidence used as the basis of assessment, and about the problematic nature of assessment (Cameron-Jones, 1987, pp. 158–159).

It seems clear that if the goal is to produce a reflective practitioner, then the student must be more involved in assessment and the focus of assessment must expand. This means a move towards a more radical approach which uses profiling, where the student's self-appraisal is taken seriously, and where assessment becomes a continuing process of reporting on all aspects of the practice: cognitive and affective; successes and failures; strengths and weaknesses; processes as well as products; deliberative and reflective abilities as well as teaching performance. Such a profile would also provide the employing school with information which would enable them better to support the probationer. (See DES, 1988b, para 1.42, p. 11.)

If the focus of assessment is now to be on the student's potential continuously to investigate, deliberate upon, and refine her practice, then supervisors and student together need to bring their multiple perspectives to considering the quality of her investigations, reflections, and deliberations upon her present practice. And these can be sampled by reading written reflections, engaging her in deliberation and observing subsequent practice and the deliberations related to it.

The processes here include continuously re-establishing the criteria between student and supervisors *as a necessary basis of the partnership of supervision*. This should afford some learning to all parties involved and, arguably, might usefully be recorded. This is not a matter of 're-inventing the wheel', but of enabling its users to get to know better the processes of learning through practice, and to make them their own. This can be accomplished by each group of student and supervisors grappling with and discussing openly the problems of trying to put a system of assessment into practice. The student's contribution to this exploration might itself be a factor in the assessment of her progress towards becoming a reflective and deliberative practitioner.

There is much work to be done here. A start might be made by summarising what a deliberative approach to sustained experience might involve.

Deliberative supervision

Rediscovering theory

Perhaps the most important aspect of deliberative supervision is the reconceptualisation of theory itself. By contrast to the notion of applying Educational Theory to practice which lay vaguely behind the almost atheoretical approaches to the supervision of practice as described in Chapter 11, this approach gives a central place to theory. But it is theory of a rather different kind. Deliberative supervision is guided by curriculum theory rather than Education Theory.

By subscribing to the approach of curriculum research rather than educational research, the view of, and emphasis on, theory is shifted in the following five crucial ways:

1. The student is actively involved in the *production* of her own theory, which means that she is actively involved in working out her own solutions from the start of teaching.
2. She must learn, in addition to the more traditional aspects of her course,

the procedures of reflection, deliberation, and investigation.
3. She must look more closely at herself and her own beliefs and values, as well as her abilities, capacities, skills, and dispositions, since in trying to understand and solve practical problems we are influenced by how we perceive those problems.
4. This will ensure that her solutions to her problems are her own and not those of her supervisors.
5. The theory produced will be the product of systematic enquiry, *aided* by, but not hijacked by insights from formal Education Theory.

The implications of this for the student and her supervisors are extensive, and will alter the content of the teacher-training curriculum. The processes of deliberation will have to be taught and the processes of and the insights of curriculum research will need to be given more consideration, and the distinctions between educational and curriculum research will have to be understood. More significantly, the implications for the supervisors will lead to a recasting of their partnership.

Recasting supervision

Following the arguments rehearsed above, it would seem that the student needs from a supervisor the following kinds of expertise:

1. expertise in educational studies, observation techniques and Educational Theory, and curriculum research
2. some experience of operating as a facilitator of students' learning across a range of classes and schools and pupils
3. intimate knowledge of the student's whole course and the context of current initial training
4. expertise in the particular school and classroom in which the practice takes place
5. expertise in the processes of reflection upon practice
6. expertise in the processes of deliberation
7. expertise in the disciplines which the student is teaching
8. expertise in practical problem-solving in and for the classroom.

The vital question then for each individual partnership group is: how might these be best provided by the supervisors? And how might these approaches themselves be continuously refined? In other words, within a framework of what is needed for the enterprise, the responsibility for dividing up these tasks becomes the partners'. Such an approach will continually offer all those involved new insights into their own work and into the processes of teaching and learning. In this way, too, it prepares the student for a professional career in which she is continuously involved in the development of her own practice and the improvement of her pupils' learning, and places her in a good position to take responsibility for the learning of other students, when she becomes a teacher.

Reshaping the post-lesson conference

Clearly, the central activities in enabling the student to learn through practice are the pre-lesson tutorials in which the above issues are explored, and the post-lesson conference or debriefing.

Some processes of debriefing have been described above. Yet there still remains much work to be done here. Various research has shown the inadequacy of both tutor and teacher in drawing the student to reflect upon the TP lesson. Mansfield (1986) reports great difficulty in raising the level of analysis of the post-lesson conference, and demonstrates that neither tutors nor teachers in his research group had an adequate model or framework for analysis. Cronshaw (1986) proposes a model of four levels of analysis for the post-lesson conference. He suggests that the supervisor considers in turn:

1. Those issues to do with survival (essentially class control matters).
2. Those concerned with details of teaching style, methods of organisation.
3. What he calls 'professional details of why things are done' (ie, deliberation upon the ends rather than the means).
4. Consideration of the context of the lesson.

This list is useful to an extent, but does not come to grips with exactly *how* to promote this kind of thinking in the student.

A similar model, which also does not come to grips with the finer detail but which is useful, is proposed by Zeichner and Lister (1985). They also argue for four levels of activity in the post-lesson conference. The first three of them are similar to Cronshaw's, but the fourth is very different and particularly useful. They distinguish:

1. Factual discourse, concerned with what has occurred in the teaching situation or what will occur in future. (This seems to subsume Cronshaw's first two.)
2. Prudential discourse, involving discussion of what to do or how to evaluate what has been accomplished. (This seems to be part of the first two of Cronshaw's points.)
3. Justificatory discourse involving consideration of the reasons why things are done. (This is the same as Cronshaw's third point.)
4. Critical discourse which examines and assesses the adequacy of reasons offered for the justification of the pedagogical actions, assesses the values and assumptions embedded in the form and content of the curriculum offered and the activities used. (This seems to be the most crucial level of all in terms of learning from the reflection. In some ways the procedures for reflection suggested above offer help with this last level.)

Some of the areas not yet fully explored in terms of deliberation and of TP include the following questions:

— how is the student's teaching planned?
— how might the teacher, tutor, and student arrive at a common under-

standing of the purpose of the TP?
- how does the supervisory team organise its tasks?
- how do the teacher, tutor, and student use their common understandings and their separate expertise to work on the student's practice?

But this is to anticipate the proposals which follow.

Conclusions: Refocusing the Challenge

13. Towards an Agenda for Action: Some Proposals

Summary

- For individual partnerships: some agenda items
  — re-establishing the partnership
  — focusing the enterprise
  — setting an agenda
  — sharing discoveries
- For the practical placement: some suggestions
  — accepting the challenge
  — recognising the advantages
  — exploring the opportunities
  — formulating a policy
- For the training institutions: some ways ahead
  — small-scale practitioner research
  — more major research
  — possibilities for award-bearing courses
- For the future: working on a broader front
  — recognising a common basis
  — developing a Professional Training Unit

Introduction

Proposals are here offered for a range of enterprises which would extend our understanding of learning through practice, and which might be tackled by the student and supervisors on the one hand, or by whole higher education institutions on the other. The suggestions are made as much from the intention of stimulating readers to create ways forward as with the intention of arguing for these specific ideas.

For individual partnerships: some agenda items

Re-establishing the partnership

The partnership of teacher, tutor, and student on sustained and intermittent school experience, or of licensed teacher and supervisor on school placement, is likely to be set up in the first place by bureaucratic means, and is bound to result in partners who have never previously met. Time and thought need to be given to re-establishing the partnership on every occasion a new team is formed, and will pay dividends. All partners will need to seek common ground in terms of the specific intentions of the partnership. Partners will need to take account of the published intentions of the training course or system. They will need to reflect upon their views on training, teaching, and learning, and they will need to acknowledge the specific contributions each individual partner can make to the enterprise in hand. As part of this important exercise, the constraints of the particular context of the partnership will also need to be weighed up carefully and openly by all parties. This will help to ensure that the declared intentions of the partners are feasible. In all of this, what is most needed is a willingness to challenge the implicit assumptions in traditional and unquestioned activities and ideas, and thus to replace habit and instinct with insight.

Focusing the enterprise

The basic intention of the school experience will, very properly, have been set by the training institution, or training system, with regard to the relationship of the placement to the rest of the course. But, within these broad intentions, there is considerable value for the individual partnership in refocusing the enterprise and reinterpreting the purpose. It is here that the partners make the enterprise their own. This is where the activities of the practice can be given a more meaningful framework by being seen as essentially investigative, reflective, and deliberative. It is here that the implications of this focus, for each partner, can be assessed, and it is here that a specific agenda for the practice can be agreed *for each partner*.

The time that this exercise will take may well save much more time spent in disentangling misunderstandings later.

Setting the agenda

If the framework of the practice is broadly that of practitioner enquiry, and if the constraints and possibilities of the situation have been reviewed, then it becomes a fairly simple matter to establish and agree together the role that each will play. Further, if each partner is engaged in investigating his/her own part in the practical activity as well as being committed to helping and advising the other partners, an atmosphere of mutual support and interest will be quickly built up. The impetus of this will be sustained as long as all parties continue to compare notes.

Sharing discoveries

The sharing of ideas and responses to situations is considerably helped by all parties keeping brief diaries. The trainee will, of course, be required to keep detailed written notes, including preparation and self-appraisal. On initial training courses these can act as a running dialogue between the student, teacher, and tutor if both contribute written comments to the student's log.

This can be done quite informally and briefly by actually writing alongside the student's work, providing that the student sees her log as an informal record. Or it can be done separately. The important issue, however, is that these notes are shared, and are about the investigation of practice, the response to it, and reflections upon it. Since oral discussion and reflection is also useful, it is worth scheduling brief meetings at which all three partners can be present as a way of monitoring the enterprise. It is important to see these as monitoring the processes involved rather than monitoring the student.

For the practical placement: some suggestions

The issues for the school placement to which the student is sent for practical professional training are equally significant. They too involve the institution accepting the challenge of partnership as outlined above, recognising the advantages to its own workings and its own staff of being thus involved, exploring the opportunities available, and formulating a policy.

Accepting the challenge

The challenge for the placement in being involved in fostering the learning of trainees on practice is a major and an extensive one. In some way or another every member of staff in the receiving institution will be affected by and will affect the student's training. Given the present level of demands upon schools, and the present attitudes of the professional work-forces in them, it seems unlikely that every institution will wish to be involved in training.

Given, too, the current need for much closer liaison between the training institution and the school placement, it seems likely that fewer establishments will need to be involved but that these will need to be more heavily involved than before. The notion of 'training schools' rears its head from time to time in this respect, and it is not unlikely that in the future we shall move more in that direction.

It therefore needs to be a major decision by the school to be involved in training, and not, as in the past, a matter of accepting yet another demand without considering the implications. If an establishment does accept this challenge, then, it ought to do so on a contractual basis. There are reciprocal responsibilities and rights in this matter. This brings with it the questions: what will it gain, and what will it have to offer?

Recognising the advantages

Clearly the key advantage to the school will be in the opportunity for staff to investigate, reflect upon, and deliberate about practice. Although at first such activities will be centred around the student's practice and the fostering of her learning from it, this deepening engagement with understanding practical matters will inevitably affect all of the practitioner's own work.

How, then, might an institution proceed if it has decided to accept the challenge?

Exploring the opportunities

In spite of the fact that the institution has received students in the past, the challenge to the partners in professional training is such that a core of staff may need to come together to assess the advantages, explore the opportunities, consider the strengths and weaknesses of the staff and the establishment, and to define its possible role in training, including its rights and responsibilities. It may well need to do this in liaison with the training institution. As a result of this not inconsiderable work, a proper policy for professional training may then be able to be articulated within the establishment. There is an agenda here for the GRIST-funded, school-based INSET.

Formulating a policy

Such a policy will need to take account of the macro and the micro decisions that have to be made when an establishment involves itself in the kind of investigative and reflective approach to training. That is, there may need to be policy decisions about how many staff may be involved at any one time, who these should be and on what basis they should be chosen, how the establishment will organise itself in terms of time and resources in order to facilitate the work of training, and what training or support the staff involved may require and how their experiences might be shared with colleagues. There may also be a need to review the organisation of liaison with the training institution, and to rethink the processes of inducting the student into the school.

If these are the new demands made upon the placement by the challenge to the partners in training, what will now be asked of the training institutions?

For the training institutions: some ways ahead

The role of the training institutions in fostering this kind of professional training seems fairly clear, whatever the actual training system for the 1990s. There is a need to help establish and support the tradition of small-scale practitioner research which will be the basis of the work of all partnerships; there is a need to set up more large-scale research to investigate those aspects of learning through practice about which we know little; and there is a need to organise courses (preferably award-bearing courses) for the partners.

Small-scale practitioner research

Small-scale practitioner research can be established by both tutors and teachers and may be carried out, and supported, in a number of ways. It may be the focus of an award-bearing course, or it may be the extension of previous action research techniques learnt on previous courses. It may be fostered by occasional workshop sessions in which a number of partnerships report back and further reflect upon their findings. Such reflection too may be offered a wider audience via publication.

But in all of this, it is important that the practitioner and tutor know that their respective establishments value and acknowledge their efforts. The attitude of those establishments will be most clearly conveyed in the priorities which they accord this work in terms of resources. This is a matter of how establishments see the enterprise of professional training.

More major research

The possibilities for further major research in the area are very considerable. One possible approach would be simply to harness and focus the investigative work of a number of partnerships. In this case, it would be necessary to set up a proper structure which supported this work, involving a properly coordinated approach to inquiry, and a systematic reporting and interpretation. A vast number of the issues raised in this book, which have never been properly investigated on any scale, could be pursued in this way.

Other possibilities for research within the institutions are also considerable. These could include enquiry into the processes of learning from practice, the debriefing processes and discussion seminars, pursuit of issues in the relationship of theory and practice, further work on practitioner's decision-making, further work on the role of observation. Much of it would have the advantage of being able to draw upon a wide range of perspectives on practice by using the work of the partners.

Here, in particular, there is scope for building upon the current investigation of ways of improving the quality of reflection-in-action in students in training. Here, important work includes that of Zeichner and Lister (1985) in America and of MacKinnon (1987) in Canada, as well as that of Terrell, Mathis, Winstanley and Wright (1986) at Cheltenham, and Cameron-Jones (1988) at Moray House. All of this work contains ideas for and experience of looking at reflection in initial training students. Coupled with, say, various approaches to analysing the language of discourse, all of this could prove useful in improving our theory and practice.

Possibilities for award-bearing courses

One further direction for the future is, clearly, the need to train teachers and tutors (or future supervisors) in these ways of working. There are good arguments for courses for supervisors, and these ought to be both award-bearing and action-research in focus. It might well be possible for these to function at master's degree level (indeed, such courses already exist), and for the supervision of initial training students or licensed teachers to be a major activity in this course. Such a course would be useful for practitioners who might then return to school as key members of a core team of trainers. Such practitioners would also be well equipped to turn to posts in training institutions, or within a new training system. But it might also be useful for new tutors currently joining a training institution from practice as a major means of inducting them into an important and new aspect of their posts.

So far all of the proposals made have been aimed at teachers and tutors. But there is also much to be said for looking at a means of bringing these professions together *across* the professional boundaries.

For the future: working on a broader front

Recognising a common basis

One of the more comforting aspects of the new demands upon training and trainers is that they are shared by many professions, and are not simply the manifestation of something wrong with one alone. All of the pressures and demands, together with the common needs, are felt across the teaching, paramedical, nursing, police, and social service professions. For all of these, too, there is a need to harness more closely theory and practice, and to improve training by improving the ways in which we foster learning through practice. This means that the professions have much to gain and much to offer each other in sharing understandings about such matters. If this approach is beginning to be demanded by the professions, the public and even governments in their calls for appraisal and evaluation, the question remains, how can learning through practice best be fostered?

Developing a Professional Training Unit

One possibility for putting into practice the above suggestions is to establish a research unit in professional training. One of the most obvious places for such a base would be in those colleges of higher education which offer a range of courses in professional training. Such establishments also have staff of their own in need of this very training – that is, staff *within* the college and staff in the professions outside the college who already help with the training, but are themselves in need of further training.

Such a unit might have five aims:

1. To promote research *across a whole institute of higher education* on matters relating to the practical professional *training and supervision* of a whole range of professional practitioners (teachers, occupational therapists, physiotherapists, nurses, social workers, and even the police).
    The term 'practical professional training and supervision' would include:
    — pedagogical aspects of training itself (initial (pre-service) and in-service)
    — the initial training curriculum and what it should contain
    — the supervision of practice on initial training placements, and the training and curriculum for such supervisors
    — the continuing development of practical skills at post-initial training level.
2. To promote, encourage, and support small-scale research by local professional practitioners into their own practice (in the terms above), leading to a range of local certificates. These could be part of an ongoing development for those teachers who wished to pursue issues raised by

the various training demands for the 1988 Education Reform Act. (It would also be one way of catering for the probable increase of requests, in the light of new INSET funding, for higher education's certification of LEA and school-based in-service work.)
3. To offer a research-oriented qualification in professional training – a BPhil or a Master's degree, depending on a student's ability and entry qualifications. (Again, these might take account of point 2 above.) This BPhil/MA could be offered to *trainers and supervisors* across all of the above categories, with a view to maintaining the balance of as many different professions as possible in each student group. The curriculum for the course at both levels (BPhil and MA) would be threefold (a choice from):
    — pedagogy for professional training (initial and in-service)
    — curriculum for professional training (initial and in-service)
    — supervision and the issues involved in learning from practice on initial training and involved in facilitating, supervising, and assessing that learning
    — issues involved in the overseeing and assessing of continuing professional development for the practitioner.
4. To accept small-scale research commissions from the local community into professional practical training, and to use these commissions as part of the degree course assessment procedures as practical coursework or dissertation work for interested students at an appropriate level and with appropriate supervision.
5. To accept, as capacity allowed, large-scale, research-oriented consultancy work for the range of practical professional training in the local community.

The unit itself would be a means of addressing together the five aims above which are mutually supportive and would benefit enormously from being developed together.

In a world in which professionalism and partnership are such important concepts, it is to be hoped that the challenges implicit in the ideas here presented will be met in the spirit in which they are offered. If we do not go forward together, we may not go forward at all.

Addenda

* *The New Teacher in School* (DES, 1988b, p. 10) also indicates concern with classroom management and control, lesson planning, matching work to abilities, questioning skills and assessment. It declares, coyly, that attention should be given during training to defining the levels of competence in skills which teachers should have by the end of their training. (In the light of this, it is ironic that the School Teachers Pay and Conditions Document (DES, 1987, pp. 23–5) lists teaching as only one of 12 sections under 'Professional duties'.)

† In the more recent survey, *The New Teacher in School* (DES, 1986b) just over a third of the 297 teachers seen thought they were well prepared to teach in a team situation.

Bibliography

Alexander, R (1984) *Primary Teaching*, London: Holt, Rinehart & Winston
Alexander, R and Whittaker, J (eds) (1980) *Developments in PGCE Courses*, Guildford: Society for Research into Higher Education
Ashton, P et al. (1983) *Teacher Education in the Classroom: Initial and In-service*, London: Croom Helm
ATCDE (1964) *Evidence to the Central Advisory Council for Education*, London: ATCDE
Barrow, R (1984) *Giving Teaching Back to Teachers*, London: Wheatsheaf
Biott, C (1983) 'The foundations of classroom action-research in initial training', *Journal of Education for Teaching*, Vol 9, No 2, pp. 152–160
Boud, D, Keogh, R and Walker, D (eds) (1985) *Reflection: Turning Experience into Learning*, London: Kogan Page
Britton, E (1969) 'The Teaching Profession and the Education of Teachers', in Taylor, W (ed) (1969)
Browne, JD (1969) 'The Balance of Studies in Colleges of Education', in Taylor, W (ed) (1969)
Busher, H, Clarke, S and Taggart, L (1988) 'Beginning Teachers' Learning', in Calderhead, J (ed) (1988)
Calderhead, J (ed) (1988) *Teachers' Professional Learning*, Lewes: Falmer
Cameron-Jones, M (1987) 'Improving Professional Practice in the Primary School', in Delamont, S (ed) (1987)
Cameron-Jones, M (1988) *Helping Students Learn Professional Practice*, Edinburgh: CNAA Primary Placement Project
Carr, W and Kemmis, S (1986) *Becoming Critical: Education, Knowledge and Action Research*, Lewes: Falmer
Clark, C (1979) 'Education and Behaviour Modification', *Journal of Philosophy of Education*, Vol 13, pp.73–81
Cronshaw, B (1986) 'An Account of the Third Phase of One College's Research Project into School Practice Supervision', in Terrell, C, Mathis, J, Winstanley, R and Wright, D (eds) (1986) pp.117–124
Delamont, S (ed) (1987) *The Primary School Teacher*, Lewes: Falmer
DES (1981) *Teacher Training and the Secondary School: The Implications of the HMI National Secondary Survey*, London: HMSO
DES (1982) *The New Teacher in School*, London: HMSO

DES (1983a) *Teaching in Schools: The Content of Initial Training*, London: HMSO
DES (1983b) *Administrative Memorandum 1/83: The Treatment and Assessment of Probationary Teachers*, London: DES
DES (1984) *Circular 3/84: Initial Teacher Training: Approval of Courses*, London: HMSO
DES (1985) *Quality in Schools: Evaluation and Appraisal*, London: HMSO
DES (1986) *CATENOTE 4: Links Between Initial Training Institutions and Schools*, London: HMSO
DES (1987) *School Teachers' Pay and Conditions Document*, London: HMSO
DES (1988a) *Qualified Teacher Status*, London: DES
DES (1988b) *The New Teacher in School: A Survey by HMI in England and Wales 1987*, London: HMSO
Dewey, J (1933) *How We Think: A Restatement of the Relation of Reflective Thinking to the Educative Process*, London: D C Heath & Co
Eisner, E (1983) 'The Art and Craft of Teaching', *Educational Leadership*, Vol 40, pp.4–13
Eisner, E (1985) *The Art of Educational Evaluation: A Personal View*, Lewes: Falmer
Fish, D (1987) 'The Initial Training Curriculum' in Golby, M (ed) *Perspectives on the National Curriculum*, Perspectives 32, Exeter: University of Exeter
Fish, D (ed) (1988) *Turning Teaching into Learning: TRIST and the Development of Professional Practice*, London: West London Press
Golby, M et al. (eds) (1975) *Curriculum Design*, London: Croom Helm
Golby, M (1976) 'Curriculum Studies and Education for Teaching', *Education for Teaching*, No 100, London: ATCDE, pp.3–9
Golby, M (1986) 'Collaborative Education: A Commentary' in Carre, C (ed) (1986) *Collaborative Teacher Education*, Perspectives 25, Exeter: University of Exeter
Golby, M (ed) (1987) *Perspectives on the National Curriculum*, Perspectives 32, Exeter: University of Exeter
Goldhammer, R (1969) *Clinical Supervision: Special Methods for the Supervision of Teachers*, London: Holt, Rinehart & Winston
Goodings, R, Bryam, M and McPartland, M (eds) (1982) *Changing Priorities in Teacher Education*, London: Croom Helm
Goodlad, S (1984) *Education for the Professions*, Guildford: SRHE and NFER
Grundy, S (1987) *Curriculum: Product or Praxis?*, Lewes: Falmer
Harris, I (1986) 'Communicating the Character of Deliberation', *Journal of Curriculum Studies*, Vol 18, No 2, pp.115–132
Hatton, Elizabeth (1985) 'Team Teaching and Teacher Orientation to Work: Implications for the PreService and InService Preparation of Teachers', *Journal of Education for Teaching*, Vol 11, No 3, pp.228–244
Hirst, P (1976) 'The PGCE Course: Its Objectives and their Nature', *British Journal of Teacher Education*, Vol 2, No 1, pp.7–22
Hirst, P (1980) 'The PGCE Course and the Training of Specialist Teachers for Secondary Schools', *British Journal of Teacher Education*, Vol 6, No 1, pp.3–21
HMSO (1972) *Teacher Education and Training* (The James Report), London: HMSO

HMSO (1978) *Primary Education in England: A Survey by HMI*, London: HMSO
HMSO (1979) *Aspects of Secondary Education in England: A Survey by HMI*, London: HMSO
HMSO (1983) *Teaching Quality*, London: HMSO
HMSO (1987) *The Third Report of the House of Commons Committee on Education, Science and the Arts*, London: HMSO
Hopkins, D and Reid, K (eds) (1985) *Rethinking Teacher Education*, London: Croom Helm
Hoyle, E (1974) 'Professionality, Professionalism and the Control of Teaching', *London Educational Review*, Vol 3, No 2, Summer 1974, pp. 13–19
Jones, A (1985) 'Tomorrow's Schools: Closed or Open?', *Journal of the Royal Society of Arts*, Vol CXXXIII, No 5347, London: RSA, pp.451–458
Kerry, T (1980) 'The Nottingham Teacher Education Project', in Alexander, R and Whittaker, J (eds) (1980)
Knitter, W (1985) 'Curriculum Deliberation: Pluaralism and the Practical', *Journal of Curriculum Studies*, Vol 17, No 4, pp.383–395
Langford, G (1978) *Teaching as a Profession: An Essay in the Philosophy of Education*, Manchester: Manchester University Press
Langford, G (1985) *Education, Persons and Society: A Philosophical Enquiry*, London: Macmillan
MacDonald-Ross, M (1975) 'Behavioural Objectives: A Critical Review', in Golby, M et al. (eds) (1975)
MacKinnon, A (1987) 'Detecting Reflection-in-action among Pre-service Elementary Science Teachers', *Teaching and Teacher Education*, Vol 3, No 2, pp. 135–145
Mansfield, P (1986) 'Patchwork Pedagogy: A Case Study of Supervisors' Emphasis in Pedagogy in Post-lesson Conferences', in Terrell, C, Mathis, J, Winstanley, R and Wright, D (1986)
McCulloch, M (1979) *School Experience in Initial BEd/BEd Honours Degrees validated by CNAA*, London: CNAA
McIntyre, D (1988) 'Designing a Teacher Education Curriculum from Research and Theory on Teacher Knowledge', in Calderhead, J (ed) (1988)
Moore J and Mattaliano, A (1970) cited in Smyth, J (ed) (1986)
NATFHE (1983) *Teacher Education – Current Issues*, London: NATFHE
Nias, J (1988) 'Introduction', in Nias, J and Groundwater-Smith, S (eds) (1988)
Nias, J and Groundwater-Smith, S (eds) (1988) *The Enquiring Teacher*, Lewes: Falmer
Passmore, J (1980) *The Philosophy of Teaching*, London: Duckworth
Pereira, P (1984) 'Deliberation and the Arts of Perception', *Journal of Curriculum Studies*, Vol 16, No 4, pp. 347–366
Pinar, W (1986) '"Whole, Bright, Deep with Understanding" Issues in Qualitative Research and Autobiographical Method', in Taylor, P H (ed) (1986), Windsor: NFER/Nelson
Pollard, A and Tann, S (1987) *Reflective Teaching in the Primary School*, London: Cassell

Reid, W (1978) *Thinking About the Curriculum: The Nature and Treatment of Curriculum Problems,* London: Routledge & Kegan Paul

Roby, T (1986) 'Habits Impeding Deliberation', in Taylor, P H (ed) (1986)

Rowland, S (1984) *The Enquiring Classroom: An Introduction to Children's Learning,* Lewes: Falmer

Rudduck, J and Sigsworth, A (1985) 'Partnership Supervision', in Hopkins, D and Reid, K (eds) (1985)

Ryle, G (1949) *The Concept of Mind,* Harmondsworth: Penguin

Schön, D (1983) *The Reflective Practitioner,* New York: Basic Books

Schön, D (1987a) 'Changing Patterns of Inquiry in Work and Living' (The Thomas Cubitt Lecture), *Journal of the Royal Society of Arts,* Vol CXXXV, No 5367, pp.226–233

Schön, D (1987b) *Educating the Reflective Practitioner,* London: Jossey-Bass

Schwab, J (1978) 'The Practical: A Language for Curriculum', in Westbury, I and Wilkoff, N (eds) (1978) *Science, Curriculum and Liberal Education: Selected Essays of J J Schwab,* Chicago: Chicago University Press

Smyth, J (1984) 'Teachers as Collaborative Learners in Clinical Supervision: A State of the Art Review', *Journal of Education for Teaching,* Vol 10, No 1, pp.24–38

Smyth, J (1985) 'Developing a Critical Practice of Clinical Supervision', *Journal of Curriculum Studies,* Vol 17, No 1, pp.1–15

Smyth, J (ed) (1986) *Learning About Teaching Through Clinical Supervision,* London: Croom Helm

Smyth, J (ed) (1987) *Educating Teachers: Changing the Nature of Pedagogical Knowledge,* Lewes: Falmer

Stenhouse, L (1975) *An Introduction to Curriculum Research and Development,* London: Heinemann

Stenhouse, L (1980) 'Artistry and Teaching: The Teacher as the Focus of Research and Development', in Hopkins, D and Wideen, M (eds) (1984) *Alternative Perspectives on School Improvement,* Lewes: Falmer

Stones, E (1979) *Psychopedagogy: Psychological Theory and the Practice of Teaching,* London: Methuen

Stones, E (1983) 'Perspectives in Pedagogy', *Journal of Education for Teaching,* Vol 9, No 1, pp.68–76

Stones, E (1984) *Supervision in Teacher Education: A Counselling and Pedagogical Approach,* London: Methuen

Sutton, C (1975) 'Theory in the Classroom', *British Journal of Teacher Education,* Vol 1, No 3, pp.335–349

Taylor, P H (ed) (1986) *Recent Developments in Curriculum Studies,* Windsor: NFER/Nelson

Taylor, W (ed) (1969) *Towards a Policy for the Education of Teachers: Proceedings of the Twentieth Symposium of the Colston Research Society,* London: Butterworth

Terrell, C, Mathis, J, Winstanley, R and Wright, D (1986) *Teaching Practice Supervision in Primary Schools,* Cheltenham: The College of St Paul and St Mary

Terrell, C, Tregaskis, O and Boydell, D (1986) Teaching Practice Supervisors in Primary Schools: An Ethnomethodological Perspective', in Terrell, C et al. (eds) (1986)

Tickle, L (1987) *Learning Teaching, Teaching Teaching . . .: A Study of Partnership in Teacher Education*, Lewes: Falmer

Tom, A (1987) 'Replacing Pedagogical Knowledge with Pedagogical Questions', in Smyth, J (ed) (1987)

Webb, D and Wilkinson, M (1980) 'Theory into Practice or Practice into Theory?' in Alexander, R and Whittaker, J (eds) (1980)

Wilson, J (1975) *Educational Theory and the Preparation of Teachers*, Windsor: NFER

Woods, P (1987) 'Life Histories and Teacher Knowledge', in Smyth, J (ed) (1987)

Zeichner, K (1986) 'Content and contexts: neglected elements in studies of student teaching as an occasion for learning to teach', *Journal of Education for Teaching*, Vol 12, No 1, pp.5–24

Zeichner, K and Lister, D (1985) 'Varieties of Discourse in Supervisory Conferences', *Teaching and Teacher Education*, Vol 1, No 2, pp.155–174